WHO IS THE REAL GOD?

MICHAEL HILL

Avid Readers Publishing Group
Lakewood, California

The opinions expressed in this manuscript are those of the author and do not represent the thoughts or opinions of the publisher. The author warrants and represents that he has the legal right to publish or own all material in this book. If you find a discrepancy, contact the publisher at www.avidreaderspg.com.

Who Is the Real God?

All Rights Reserved

Copyright © 2018 Michael Hill

This book may not be transmitted, reproduced, or stored in part or in whole by any means without the express written consent of the publisher except for brief quotations in articles and reviews.

Avid Readers Publishing Group

http://www.avidreaderspg.com

ISBN-13: 978-1-61286-354-2

Library of Congress Control Number: 2018965150

Printed in the United States

DEDICATION

This book is dedicated to the agnostics and atheists of this world who after having read the Bible are confused and have consequently lost their faith. Unfortunately, the gods in the Old Testament give God a bad name.

Hopefully, this book will help those who still have an open mind to realize that there really is a God.

ACKNOWLEDGMENT

I would like to thank my sister, Pat Hill, for her invaluable input and proof reading the original manuscript.

I would also like to thank my wife, Lynne, for her never-ending and enthusiastic support of everything I have attempted to accomplish.

Lastly, but certainly not least, I would like to thank my oldest grandson, Trevor Miller, for his invaluable help in creating the picture file.

TABLE OF CONTENTS

INTRODUCTION	vii
CHAPTER 1: THE EXISTENCE OF GOD	1
CHAPTER 2: THE QUEST BEGINS	16
CHAPTER 3: THE "GODS"	19
CHAPTER 4: OTHER INTELLIGENT LIFE	28
CHAPTER 5: THE VATICAN LIBRARY	36
CHAPTER 6: ADAM & EVE AND CAIN & ABEL	38
CHAPTER 7: THE NEPHILIM	40
CHAPTER 8: ENOCH	42
CHAPTER 9: NOAH AND THE GREAT FLOOD	48
CHAPTER 10: SODOM AND GOMORRAH	54
CHAPTER 11: MOSES AND THE ARK OF THE COVENANT	57
CHAPTER 12: TOWER OF BABEL	60
CHAPTER 13: EZEKIEL'S VISION	63
CHAPTER 14: BIRTH OF JESUS CHRIST	64

CHAPTER 15: CHRONOLOGY	67
CHAPTER 16: RULES AND LAWS BEFORE THE TEN COMMANDMENTS	72
CHAPTER 17: THE FACE OF GOD	74
CHAPTER 18: THE CREATION OF THE UNIVERSE	78
CHAPTER 19: THE EVIDENCE OR MYSTERIES	82
CHAPTER 20: ANALYSIS, SPECULATION & CONCLUSIONS	128
CHAPTER 21: THE MEANING OF LIFE	147
CHAPTER 22: HEAVEN	152
EPILOGUE	158

INTRODUCTION

It all started **nine billion years ago** with the **"Big Bang"**, but for me it all started **nine years ago** on the day that I retired from a 40-year career of helping turn around and growing a number of manufacturing companies. With a formal education in both Business and Operations Research Engineering, which included two master degrees, I spent very little time reading anything other than business and engineering related books during my career; so immediately upon retirement I embarked on a quest to **seek an understanding of the meaning of life**. Unexpectedly, however, my quest immediately took a major detour and quickly headed in an unforeseen direction, which is the main subject of this book.

I started by reading the Bible, but found the Old Testament too difficult to read (**wild examples to follow**) and wasn't answering any of my questions to better understand life. In fact, **I had more questions than answers,** which led my quest to finding possible answers to those questions. The New Testament on the other hand was a lot more understandable but only reinforced my beliefs that I had already embraced during my 12 year Catholic education from both nuns in grade school and Franciscan priests in high school.

I was far from a religious scholar in grade school, which was taught by nuns. As an example, at the age of 8 we were all required to memorize the Act of Contrition by rote, which I could easily recite. For those of you not familiar with this prayer, it starts like this: **"Oh my God I am heartily sorry for having offended thee."** Well to test our ability to correctly memorize this prayer we were required to put it in writing. Several days later, the nun who had graded this test proceeded to announce to the class that "Mr. Hill (yes, that's me) has apparently found what he thinks is an easier way to get to heaven". Well when you're only 8 and your teacher refers to you as "Mr." you instantly know that what is coming next will not be good. She then read my paper out loud to the class **"Oh my God I am partly sorry for having offended thee"**. "Sounded" good to me. In any event, 55 short years later I dusted myself off and was finally ready to start anew.

In writing this book I decided that in order to be open minded and also an honest broker, **I must play devil's advocate**, despite the fact that I may risk offending those of faith. I clearly recognize this risk because I too am a person of deep faith. Having said that, this book may actually strengthen the faith of those who have always accepted their faith despite having had some lingering doubts or questions. **It is the purpose of this book to raise provocative questions and then attempt to provide possible answers.**

A belief in God is a complex concept so I will be quoting credible scientists who should be respected for their intellectual scientific research and beliefs, **despite being non-believers.**

When reading this book, please don't overlook the fact that I use no less than 150 question marks (?), which are not statements of facts but rather provocative questions designed to stimulate a discussion in your mind of many possibilities, which you may or may not deem to be credible or possible.

Michael Hill

CHAPTER 1

THE EXISTENCE OF GOD

Let me start by saying that I believe that it takes an infinite amount of faith to believe that there is no God than to believe that there is a God. Some people don't believe in God because they are too confused after reading the Bible, and rightfully so because of the recorded actions of "God". Also, some **don't want to believe in God** because if God exists then they need to follow His rules or Commandments, which interferes with their self-gratification. Humans have strong desires, but we must not allow those desires to cloud our judgment when it comes to a belief in God. Some even say, **"Well, if there is a God, then He created me with these desires, so it is all God's fault that I am the way I am"; BUT**, and this is a big but, God also gave us a **Conscience and Free Will for a specific purpose,** which you will clearly understand by the end of this book.

My basic premise for this book is that there must be a God, but who is the real God? Only

after the imposter gods are unmasked will the real God be revealed.

Since I am writing this book primarily for agnostics and atheists, I feel that I owe you an explanation of why I believe in a God before I speak of unmasking the imposter gods.

The **scientific basis** for my belief in a God begins with the **Hubble telescope** and **the sophisticated coding within our DNA**, which has many scientists admitting that the universe and life appears to be part of a **grand design**.

More and more scientists believe in a "grand design" as they talk about a Creator, despite not having any personal religious belief whatsoever. This revelation stems from the **science of astronomy and molecular biology**, i.e. the universe actually had a beginning (**the Big Bang**), which happened to be perfect for life, and **DNA** reveals intelligence of absolutely unimaginable proportions.

Even though Einstein was skeptical of religious beliefs as told in the Bible, he is quoted as having said, "Everyone who is seriously involved in the pursuit of science becomes convinced that a spirit is manifest in the laws of the universe-a Spirit vastly superior to that of man."

When we view the sky with the naked eye we can see about 5,000 stars, but the **Hubble telescope** has revealed that there are **over a billion-trillion stars clustered in over 100 billion galaxies**. An absolutely astonishing revelation to say the least!

Prior to Edwin Hubble, scientists believed that the **universe had always existed and was in a static state**, but that all changed with the evidence in 1931 that the **universe is expanding**, and thus had **a beginning via the Big Bang**, which points to a Creator.

You may be asking yourself how did the scientists conclude that from an expanding universe there was a beginning and the Big Bang? Well, before the universe was proven to be expanding **it was thought to have always existed somehow and that it was not created but was just simply there.** Through the Hubble telescope it was proven that the universe was expanding, so all of the scientists had to admit that they had been wrong. In fact, **Einstein stated that believing that it had always existed was the biggest mistake of his life.**

So how does an expanding universe prove that there was a beginning and what does the Big Bang have to do with it? Well, it is really quite simple; **if something is expanding it must obviously have been smaller previously and "something must have happened" to cause it to expand and also to have formed prior to the beginning of its expansion process.** Essentially, **the beginning was a creation of something from nothing**, which was dubbed the **"Big Bang"**. Many scientists were shocked by the parallel story in Genesis in the Bible, "In the **beginning** God created the heavens and the earth", which ties into **a creation of something from nothing.**

Robert Jastrow, with a PhD in theoretical physics and a member of NASA when it was formed in 1958, was an agnostic; however, with the discovery of the Big Bang, he began to believe that there was a beginning to the universe and hence a Creator. He once said that, "Astronomers now find they have painted themselves into a corner because they have proven, by their own methods, that the world began abruptly in a act of creation to which you can trace the seeds of every star, every planet, every living thing in the cosmos and on earth. And they have found that all this happened as a product of forces they cannot hope to discover. That there are what I or anyone would call supernatural forces at work now, I think, a scientifically proven fact." He also said that, "For the scientist who has lived in the power of reason, the story ends like a bad dream. He has scaled the mountain of ignorance; he is about to conquer the highest peak; as he pulls himself over the final rock, he is greeted by a band of theologians who have been sitting there for centuries."

Likewise, another agnostic with a PhD in particle physics and Nobel Prize winner, George Smoot, stated that, "There is no doubt that a parallel exists between the Big Bang as an event and the Christian notion of creation from nothing, and if you are religious it's like looking at God."

We have all seen explosions of one sort or another in our lives, but have you ever seen an explosion produce a watch or anything else for that matter? To believe that an explosion without an intelligent design behind it could create something would be as ridiculous as believing that this book could have been produced by an explosion at a printing shop.

Scientists are in agreement that a big bang explosion would not create life unless a designer planned it. They used words to describe this designer as a "Spirit", "Super-Intellect", "Creator", and "Supreme Being". Their premise is based on the fact that the universe is uniquely and specifically designed for life, i.e. gravity and the laws of physics that govern our universe must be exactly right or otherwise it would not exist.

As an example, if the expansion rate of the universe were just ever so slightly slower, then gravity would have pulled all matter back and collapsed into a single point of mass. Stephen Hawking stated that, **"If the rate of expansion one second after the Big Bang had been smaller by even one part in a hundred thousand-million-million, the universe would have re-collapsed before it ever reached its present size."**

Fortunately, the universe is still expanding and it is estimated that it will not reach its zenith for another 4.5 billion years at which time it will be overtaken by gravity. There exists counter arguments to this line of thought based on the existence of black holes; however, our sun is nonetheless expected to burn out in 4.5 to 5 billion years from now anyway, so the state of the universe 4.5 billion years from now is somewhat academic for us and should not cause a loss of sleep.

Conversely, had the expansion rate been a mere fraction greater than it was, then all galaxies, stars and planets could never have formed, and we wouldn't be here. And for life to exist, the conditions in our solar system and our own planet also needed to be just right, i.e. an atmosphere of oxygen to breath, which is also necessary to create water that is critical or essential for life as are the other elements such as hydrogen, nitrogen, sodium, carbon, calcium and phosphorus. And this is not all that needs to be just right, like the size, temperature, relative proximity and chemical makeup of our planets, sun and moon. **Everything must have been just right for our existence.** The scientists who believe in a God readily accepted this new information; however, the atheists and agnostics were unable to explain the **remarkable "coincidences".**

One astronomer calculated the odds of life resulting from the Big Bang as being less than one chance in a trillion, trillion, trillion, trillion, trillion, trillion, trillion, trillion, trillion, trillion, trillion, trillion, trillion or **virtually absolutely impossible or zero**.

These scientific understandings led the agnostic astronomer, George Greenstein, to ask, "As we survey all the evidence, the thought insistently arises that some Supernatural Agency must be involved. Is it possible that suddenly, without intending to, we have stumbled upon the scientific proof of the existence of a Supreme Being? Was it God who stepped in and so providentially crafted the cosmos for our benefit?"

There is yet another discovery of **intelligent design**; namely, **DNA. These tiny DNA molecules have been called the brains behind each cell in our bodies, which contains over 37.2 trillion cells. This understanding is also true of all living things.** The more that scientists discover about DNA the more amazed they are at the absolute brilliance behind it.

DNA's intricate complexity caused its co-discoverer, Francis Crick, to believe that it could never have originated on earth naturally.

Crick, an evolutionist, stated that, "An honest man, armed with all of the knowledge available to us now, could only state that in some sense, the origin of life appears at the moment to be **almost a miracle**, so many are the conditions which would have had to have been satisfied to get it going."

The coding behind DNA reveals such intelligence that it is beyond mindboggling. As an example, it is estimated that a pinhead volume of DNA contains information equivalent to the information in a four-foot high stack of books that would encircle the earth 5,000 times or 120,000,000 miles; therefore, **"mindboggling" hardly begins to describe it.**

The DNA molecule points to an intelligence far exceeding what could have occurred by natural causes. Even Crick remarked, **"Natural selection could never have produced the first molecule."**

Noted atheist Antony Flew's life-long belief came to an abrupt end when he studied the remarkable intelligence behind DNA. He stated that, "What I think the DNA material has done is to show that **intelligence must have been involved** in getting these extraordinarily diverse elements together. The enormous complexity by which results were achieved look to me like the work of intelligence...It now seems to me that the finding of more than 50 years of DNA research have provided materials for a new and enormously powerful argument to design." **Flew admitted that the "software" behind DNA is far too complex to have originated without a "designer".** He started to believe in the possibility of a God because of **"the impossibility of providing a naturalist account of the origin of the first reproducing organism."**

It appears that the Bible was correct regarding the creation of the universe via the Big Bang, so is it possible that it was correct on other issues as well?

Okay, proving the existence of God may seem like a tall order; but I remember a great story from grade school that has stayed with me for over 60 years because it provided a perspective. I found it to be extremely compelling and I hope to be able to do it justice. The story went something like this:

Visualize walking along the shoreline of a beach and coming across an elegant pocket watch that had washed up onto the shore. You pick it up and start to examine it carefully. You press on the stem and the back of the watch opens revealing all of its inner workings including a multitude of gears and springs in an impressive array that operates in a magical synchrony of movement. The face of the watch is equally as impressive with it crystal dial and exacting movement of the second, minute and hour hands. Next you notice that in addition to keeping the exact time of day it actually has a small window displaying the day of the month. You quickly realize how complex this watch really is and how talented the master watchmaker must obviously be.

Now you begin to question the existence of the master watchmaker and ponder the possibility that the watchmaker doesn't exist. You then rationalize the watch was actually created by the ocean with all of its materials from sand and seaweed to seashells and algae. Then, you simply add the motion of the waves that obviously was the agent or catalyst that brought all of the component parts together albeit over possibly millions of years and presto you have a watch, right? Yes, that's the ticket. Then you come to your senses and find it impossible to conclude anything other than the fact that a master watchmaker must have created the watch.

So now we can move on to our next mystery; namely, you now start to examine the human body with all of its component parts, from the brain, mouth, eyes, ears, nose, heart, lungs, kidney, liver, nervous system, veins, muscles, joints, ligaments, blood vessels, reproductive organs, hands, feet, legs and arms, to hundreds of other body aspects, like skin, a voice box, five senses, lymph nodes, DNA etc.

You then ponder the possibility that the human body could have been created by an accident of nature, like being washed up on an ocean beach with everything properly connected and in perfect working order. Once again you come to your senses and conclude just like with the watch that the human body, infinitely more complex than the watch, must also have had a maker or creator.

I have obviously been talking about the theory of random evolution as an alternative to God having created man. Over time the evolution of the human species has evolved in many different ways. From a physical standpoint we can clearly recognize our ancestral likeness, albeit somewhat better looking today, but that is subject to debate. What is absolutely unquestionable is the evolution of our brain, which is self-evident based on an incredible leap forward in our cognitive functions and technological abilities. How and why did our brain get smarter and why did it happen so quickly? Random evolution happens extremely slowly, but instead of a steady linear progression over long periods of time, our brains actually developed almost exponentially overnight in comparison. Was a more powerful brain necessary? If so it absolutely implies a reason or special intent for a future purpose, which implies some type of intelligence behind the intent, like a creator. Highly accelerated evolution without an intelligent being behind it strains credulity, as the evolution of our brain was anything but random. Why did other species not evolve anywhere near as fast as humans? **Not even close**.

Other than the question about our brain, the biggest question I have is how did we develop the ability to speak through a random evolutionary process? Was an ability to speak necessary for a special intent for a future purpose? If so, this too implies some type of intelligence behind the intent as well. If God wanted us to have a more capable brain, then how ineffective would it be if none of us could talk? Without verbal communication it is hard to believe that we would have been able to use our newfound brainpower to accomplish all that we have accomplished, including but not limited to putting a man on the moon for example.

If God wanted to take credit for our existence He could have simply had all of the religions of the world chronicle our creation as having evolved from the apes, which He could say He created. **But He didn't.** Instead, all of the religions have chronicled an unmistakable clear-cut message that **God created us "first hand" from the get-go.** Please keep in mind that **a belief in evolution does not disprove the existence of God** but I find it absolutely impossible to embrace, as a belief in the random evolution of man would require a tremendous amount of faith. In fact, as previously stated, as far as faith goes I believe that it takes infinitely more faith to believe that there is no God than to believe that there is a God.

Additionally, I don't see a downside in believing in **a loving God**. The **benefits are many** including having an outline of what is acceptable and what is not via the Ten Commandments and other teachings in the Bible, not to mention the hope for not just a life after death but for the greatest life possible. Please note that I included the Ten Commandments as an actual **benefit** with all of its "Thou Shalt Nots". I am sure many would love to be able to pick and choose just 7 or 8 out of the 10 to obey; however, it has been my observation that life is much easier with rules that make you a better person. I don't know if there is a Hell; but, if there actually is one, it may very well be here on earth based on the personal consequences of our bad decisions, like incarceration, fines, depression, guilt, anxiety, regret etc. **Obeying rules makes for a better life that is free of guilt and other negative consequences**.

CHAPTER 2

THE QUEST BEGINS

After reading both the Old and New Testaments, I discovered a number of books (25 to be exact) that **dealt with everything from ancient civilizations and their understanding of the universe to their belief in why and how we were created**. I found these books to be extremely fascinating; but **I still remain skeptical of many of their findings**. However, one common thread that was difficult for me to shake was the fact that **almost all ancient religions and early civilizations around the world had a belief in a God, gods, or spiritual beings that were involved in our creation and subsequent development**. As an example, many ancient religions and some of the earliest civilizations believed that **"unearthly beings" played a big part in both our creation and "development" (a benevolent transfer of knowledge for our sole benefit)**. Some even believed that these spiritual beings or gods actually came to earth and had sexual relations and impregnated earthly women who subsequently gave birth to "demigods" (half man and half god). It was then these benevolent gods and demigods with their mystical powers that brought us enlightenment in everything from mathematics and agriculture to spiritual beliefs. **Wow, how crazy is this?**

Well, trying to keep an open mind about everything I was reading I realized that this belief might not be totally crazy after all. To help bridge the gap I asked myself the following questions: Was Mary (mother of Jesus) a human being? Had a spiritual being ("angel") visited Mary in her sleep as a messenger of God informing her that she would become pregnant? Did Mary give birth to Jesus the Son of God? Did Joseph, her husband, acknowledge and accept that he was not the biological father? Did Jesus have mystical powers? As strange as it may seem, this scenario is not totally unique, as many of the world's ancient religions or earliest civilizations have written records on clay tablets of similar stories of visits by "spiritual beings or gods" with the impregnation of humans and the subsequent birth of demigods with their mystical powers. Even the Bible has similar stories, which I discuss in Chapter 7. **If and only if these stories are to be believed**, then was it all part of **God's "master plan"** in helping mankind in both our discovery of knowledge and possibly with the gift of a more cognitive brain via the transfer of their DNA? **Could it be this DNA transfer that would solve the mystery of the "missing link" and counter the theory of random evolution?**

For those believers who may be upset with what I have said about Mary being impregnated, please keep in mind that I did not say that there was any sexual interaction, but conception did happen somehow, right? Well the answer is much clearer today with our modern technology of helping women who have a difficult time conceiving by the use of artificial insemination, so that is very well how it could have happened. And of course for those of faith nothing is impossible with God.

CHAPTER 3

THE "GODS"

I find it interesting that God's first Commandment says, **"Thou shalt have no other gods before me"**. It obviously implies His clear understanding that there was a belief at the time in other gods, which begs the question; why was there a belief in other gods? Who were these "other gods" that He was acknowledging and who started the concept of a belief in gods anyway?

Well, since God created all things it is obvious that He actually created the gods of which He speaks; however, He did not create them as His equal or as Gods, but rather as intelligent beings. **Were these gods actually His first creation of intelligent beings who had a greater intellect than humans**; hence their superiority to humans with an "advanced level of technology", which allowed them to **appear to us** as Gods? Could it be that these **"first creations"** then became the good and evil angels in the Bible? Could this then explain the mythical tails of the clash of the "Gods" and the reason why we have evil in the world? Could it then be these "fallen angels" that became referred to as the devil and his angels? I speak further about this subject in Chapter 7.

It has been said that we have **free will**, which would be impossible without evil because without evil there would be no need for **free will to choose between good and evil** and therefore no opportunity for growth leaving no chance to become all that God wanted us to be.

Those humans who curried favor with the gods were held in high esteem and became powerful leaders by keeping sway over their people. **To control mankind it was obvious that kingships and religions were created.** In fact, there were at least a dozen gods prior to the teachings in the Bible.

There was a constant battle in Egypt from one pharaoh to another, as some completely changed their belief system, i.e. the change from worshiping many gods to just the Sun god, with some pharaohs even claiming that they were gods. Then and until today it has become, "My

God is better than your God". Hence humanity has been in a constant state of war in the name of God, **but who is the real God?**

There were no less than three "Gods" in South America; namely, **Viracocha** (Inca), **Quetzalcoatl** (Aztec) and **Kukulkan** (Maya). Even though these gods have different descriptions, like feathered serpent or snake, they are thought to be the same god and were commonly **described as being white with a beard**, unlike the Christian God, which has no description since **no one had seen His face**.

Hundreds of North and South American Indian and South Pacific legends tell of a **white-skinned, bearded lord** who traveled among the many tribes to bring peace about **2,000 years ago. He was known as Quetzalcoatl.** I find it interesting that he was depicted as having a beard since **Indians do not have beards, so they would not know what a beard would look like unless they saw one (Fig. A)**.

Fig. A
Quetzalcoatl
(South American God)

There is also an interesting depiction of the Assyrian winged god with a beard **(Fig. B) from the other side of the world**. Do these beards look too similar to be just a coincidence? And just the fact that they had beards at all is very interesting.

Fig. B
Assyrian Winged God

This white bearded god was thought to be the Creator God and it is believed that **human beings were his second attempt** as his first were giants he had made from stone, but **they**

proved to be unruly so he punished them by sending a great flood. He then created men and women from clay. Do these stories seem a little too familiar? He departed by sailing west across the Pacific Ocean and promised to return one day. Isn't it interesting and very strange that this "God" left in any type of seafaring vessel at all? And isn't it also very interesting that there was a reference to a **great flood** that was created for a specific purpose?

Kukulkan warned the Maya of another bearded white man who would conquer them and also enforce a new religion on them before Quetzalcoatl would return and, in fact, the Aztecs thought that it was their "God" (Quetzalcoatl) that was returning in 1,519 AD with his shining body (suit of armor), but they made a huge mistake, as it was actually Cortez that they were welcoming.

From the Bible are we to believe that God was only concerned about the people who lived in and around Israel? Of course there were the 12 apostles who were charged with the task of spreading the Word of God; however, there are no records that mention or chronicle their travels to the Americas (north or south), which was highly populated at that period of time. Did God take the view adopted by the European explorers 1,500 years later that other populations were just savages? If anyone needed saving, it might well have been those savages, especially the ones who performed human sacrifices, right? Not only was it a barbaric practice but also it was counter to God's Commandment of "Thou Shalt Not Kill". It's too bad that Jesus didn't pay them a visit 1,500 years earlier. Are we to believe that it was left up to Cortez and his "missionaries" 1,500 years later to spread the Word of Christ on behalf of God in the western hemisphere? Killing or murdering people to make them believers sounds very familiar today, i.e. ISIS. After all, aren't they just following what they believe in the name of Allah (God)? Obviously, God did not send Cortez and his band of gold robbers, right?

Also, since the stories of Quetzalcoatl were from 2,000 years ago, was there some connection with Jesus arriving in the east at about the same time?

About 2,000 years ago God sent his only Son, Jesus, to save us, which begs the question;

even though the Holy Trinity (God the father, His only Son Jesus and the Holy Spirit) is all in one, why did God not simply come to earth and "handle the problem" first hand as opposed to "delegating" to His Son Jesus? Rather than having a Spiritual being (God) visit mankind, having His Son visit in a **human form** may have been deemed more relatable, especially with His dying on the cross for our salvation and His subsequent resurrection.

Even though Jesus began preaching at the age of 12, he only lived for 33 years, so why was His tenure on earth designed to be so relatively short with so much work to do? What was the rush to try to save the world in such a short period of time and with a totally limited amount of personal exposure around the world?

Two thousand years ago the world was not only considered to be flat, but the human population at the time of Jesus was considered to be only on the eastern continents. Of course, God knew otherwise. Other religious cultures around the world (western hemisphere) have recorded similar visits by a "God" that was very benevolent, but none talked of a Son of God who either died on a cross or died in any manner whatsoever in order to save them from their sins. These "Gods" simply departed and said that they would return, but just like Jesus none have yet to return.

CHAPTER 4

OTHER INTELLIGENT LIFE

Interestingly enough, in the last several years the Catholic Church has actually accepted the idea that **the universe may contain other intelligent life forms beyond our world**. I found this revelation to be extremely interesting. The Church's position is that if there are other intelligent life forms it does not in any way negate the belief in God. Every year we are learning more and more about the universe and the increased possibility of the existence of other life forms. So in the face of ever mounting evidence, it is my belief that the Church wanted to get out in front of this possibility to avoid a full-scale religious panic in the event that it does in fact become irrefutable. This brings me to the **Vatican library**, which I discuss in the next chapter. What may be in that library that has not been made public? **May they already have the proof?**

I also found it interesting (possibly crazy) to note that according to some **past NASA**

employees our government is very concerned about the possibility of mass panic if certain highly classified information were to become public. Some of these past employees could be simply labeled as kooks, but I found one "story" relative to the existence of God to be extremely provocative, i.e. **"Humans are a hybrid race and a product of other intelligent beings in the universe with some being benevolent and some not, but there actually is a God who created the universe and seeded the stars, planets and all forms of life including intelligent life forms"**.

Who knows? **Is it possible that there is a God and that He created other intelligent beings first and in turn these beings then came to earth and had a hand in our development if not our actual creation? Are we really so self-absorbed as not to keep open the possibility that we may not have been God's first and only choice for an intelligent life form?**

Is there a possibility of intelligent life on other planets? With the vastness of the universe, are we it? Considering that astrophysicists believe **that there exists in excess of a hundred**

billion galaxies, it is not only very likely but almost a certainty. And considering the age of the universe it could be very likely that they would be more technologically advanced than we are today.

One of the oldest known civilizations on earth was located in the southernmost region of ancient Mesopotamia (Modern day Iraq and Kuwait), which is generally considered the cradle of civilization. **The city was called Sumer** (In the Book of Genesis Sumer is known as Shinar). The Sumerians people left **cuneiform script writings on over thirty thousand clay tablets**, which were translated by Dr. Zecharia Sitchin (a Biblical scholar) over a 30-year period in the mid 20th century. Despite his interpretation and translation being rejected by scientists and academics, I still found his accounts of their life to be very interesting, yet I remain very skeptical. Basically, he says that extraterrestrial astronauts, which the Sumerians called the Anunnaki (meaning those who from heaven to earth came), fashioned man in **their image** and gave mankind civilization and religion.

The Anunnaki were looking to find gold for their planet and earth looked to be a great prospect; however, in order to mine this gold they needed to **create a labor force** because as astronauts they were ill suited to be miners and mutinied due to the backbreaking work. **After many debates, and despite great dissension amongst the Anunnaki regarding the sharing of their DNA with an extremely primitive life form that existed on earth many thousands of years ago, a small number of their scientists forged ahead to create a labor force.**

The dissension was based on not knowing if they **should or could** create intelligent beings using **their DNA** with these primitive life forms. Subsequently, their "experiments" resulted in the creation of a lot of defective beings that ended up breeding and multiplied in calamitous proportions, which then required a **great flood** of the Anunnaki's making to wipe out the population in order to start over again.

It is said that the Anunnaki viewed this great flood from the safety of their space station and were **absolutely horrified** by what they saw (unimaginable pain and suffering), **so they vowed to never create a great flood ever again**. The tablets also speak of everything ranging from the transfer of knowledge to conflicts between the **divided Anunnaki**, which culminated in the use of **nuclear weapons-an event recorded in the Bible as the upheaval of Sodom and Gomorrah**. I address the Bible's account of the destruction of the cities of Sodom and Gomorrah in Chapter 10.

These Sumerian tablets also included accounts of **Gilgamesh (Fig. C)** whom was a historic **King of Sumer** who ruled between 2800 and 2500 BC. The classic poem **The Epic of Gilgamesh** from the 21st century BC tells of his quest for immortality. This poem was thought to have greatly influenced the subsequent writing of **Homer's Iliad and the Odyssey**, which was written thirteen hundred years later in the 8th century BC.

Gilgamesh was a demigod with superhuman strength, however, unlike most demigods he was not half god and half human but rather $2/3^{rd}$ god and $1/3^{rd}$ human because his father was a god and his mother was a demigod. Because he was $2/3^{rd}$ god he felt that he unquestionably deserved to have the immortality that was strictly reserved for the gods by the gods and which was specifically withheld from humans.

Who Is the Real God?

Fig. C
Gilgamesh
(King of Sumer)

According to Dr. Sitchin's translation, Gilgamesh was absolutely outraged that he was not immortal like the gods and became obsessed about his own death. Consequently, he decided to confront the gods at their **"spaceport" near the Cedar Forest of Lebanon** and demand immortality, which required him to embark on a long and perilous journey. He knew of their location because he could see the flames in the dark of night from afar as the gods were constantly coming and going to and from earth. **Baalbek, Lebanon is near the Cedar Forest**. It is a detailed and extremely captivating story, which has you rooting for him because of his tenacious and many struggles, but in the end he was denied immortality and lived a life of misery contemplating his own death.

Despite the skepticism surrounding Sitchin's translations, which I had mentioned earlier, I felt compelled to include this story because of the connection to **Baalbek** as a "spaceport". I address the **mysterious megalithic structure at Baalbek, Lebanon** in Chapter 19.

Many things could have happened over hundreds of thousands of years, right? What about over millions or even billions of years?

Is it possible that a totally different intelligent creation by God happened millions or billions of years ago of which we have absolutely no knowledge or proof? The fact that we may not have any knowledge or proof of God's earlier creations doesn't mean that it didn't happen. The conundrum is that we simply do not know, so we need to search for evidence and then evaluate the evidence with our modern day technological tools and an open mind. Having said that, **we need to look at all "credible" written and physical archeological evidence**. Unfortunately, faith is not a tangible thing, but for many people (including myself) it is nonetheless a powerful belief; however, this book is on a fact-finding mission.

CHAPTER 5

THE VATICAN LIBRARY

Regarding information at the Vatican library, in the 1920's a **Russian scientist and philosopher**, Dr. Henry Ludvick, who spoke 20 modern and ancient languages, visited the Vatican library to research his interest in architecture. **He was given access to the Vatican's secret library and found manuscripts referring to alien visitors from around the world**. Lenin, whom had suppressed both religion and a belief in alien beings, subsequently had him imprisoned for decades as a spy for the Vatican. This information came to light only after the demise of the Soviet Union in 1991. Additionally, Matest Argrest, an independent Russian investigative reporter, had published articles in Russia of how **extraterrestrial aliens had visited earth** but the Soviet Union suppressed his theories as well.

It has been said that the Vatican library contains **53 miles** of shelf space. I don't know about you but I would be impressed with a half mile, but 53 miles is absolutely mindboggling. What are in those miles of records? Obviously, the information in those miles of records would be too much information to have been divulged in the Bible, so it begs the question; **what don't we know that may be in those records?**

I have learned that there were a lot of scriptures that are excluded from the Bible, in fact 14 chapters. Why were they specifically excluded? Some speculate that they were excluded because they were either too strange, didn't fit the narrative or were contradictory to other scriptures in the Bible.

CHAPTER 6

ADAM & EVE AND CAIN & ABEL

Without going into great detail of the Old Testament, which is extremely lengthy and somewhat detailed, but nonetheless can be very confusing, I will make a few brief observations and conclusions regarding **God's first creation of man**.

According to scripture, God created Adam and Eve, who subsequently had their first child, Cain. Cain killed their second child, Abel, and for this murder God exiled him. **Thus this murder reduced the world's human population from 4 to just 3 people (Adam, Eve and Cain), right?**

While exiled it is said that Cain worried that he would be killed by strangers. **These "strangers" must have been people other than Adam and Eve, right?** Soon thereafter Cain finds a wife and builds a settlement, which begs the questions; where did he find his wife and who were the people that would inhabit the settlement? Did other people exist outside of the Garden? If so, then **Adam and Eve may not have been the first humans God created**, or the only humans that existed at that time.

How could just two people begin to populate the world without incest? However, if in fact there were other humans at that time and Adam and Eve were not God's first creation, then incest may not have happened at all; and we all know that incest produces genetically defective beings.

CHAPTER 7

THE NEPHILIM

According to the Bible (Genesis in the Old Testament) the "sons of God" who became the "fallen angels" came to earth from the heavens and had sexual intercourse with humans that were the **unrighteous descendent daughters from Cain** and they had offspring, which were called the Nephilim (giants). How do you think they traveled to earth? Did they travel in some type of vehicle or did God somehow transport them to earth? In any event their offspring's (Nephilim's) behavior on earth became so bad with unnatural acts (homosexuality, sodomy and beastiality) that God decided to destroy what he had created on earth with the Great Flood. Do you think that an all-powerful God could have simply eliminated whomever He wanted with the blink of an eye and don't you think that He would have known what the "fallen angels" were going to do on earth **before they departed** and then stopped them?

Fortunately, Noah and his family were righteous people and did not have any of the Nephilim genes in their family's history, so they were

God's chosen ones to repopulate the earth. Unfortunately, some of the Nephilim survived the Great Flood, so evil was still on the earth as recorded in the subsequent story of **Sodom and Gomorrah** (the men of Sodom wanted to have sex with the male angels that were staying with Lot and his family just days before the cities were destroyed by God). This story is discussed further in Chapter 10.

The Nephilim were described in the Bible as super-sized humans (giants). Subsequent stories talk about David and Goliath (the giant) and the battle between good and evil, whereby Goliath is described as being about 11 feet tall. Could Goliath have been a Nephilim or a descendent of the Nephilim?

CHAPTER 8

ENOCH

There are stories in the Book of Genesis that describe **"fiery heavenly chariots"**, such as Enoch's encounters with God who took him up to Heaven and taught him in all fields of knowledge for the sole benefit of mankind. He prophesied the coming of Jesus and stressed the critical importance of having a lineage free of Nephilim genes so that Jesus would be born 100% man and 100% God. This is emphasized again in Chapter 14.

The fact that Enoch was the **great grandfather of Noah** who built the Ark, he obviously was born well before the Great Flood. This is also corroborated by communications regarding Noah's strange appearance as a young boy, which I discuss in the next chapter. In fact, it is said that God took Enoch for the last time when he was 365 years old, so he would have been born hundreds of years before the flood. When Enoch "was taken" by God he was not taken as in having died but rather went with God, so his life span is not known.

Interestingly, Enoch's son, Methuselah, lived to be over 900 year old. It is said in the Bible that after the Great Flood God limited our lifespan to no more than 120 years, which is exactly what we have today.

This certainly sounds very compelling, however, there is another interpretation of the 120 years; namely, God was giving mankind 120 years to become righteous people or else the Great Flood would certainly happen. This would also have given Noah 120 years to build the Ark and collect the animals, a huge undertaking. It only makes sense that it would take Noah a considerable amount of time to get ready for the Great Flood, but how were the people warned to change their ways or else pay the consequences for their evil ways? Both Enoch and Noah would certainly have played a huge part in educating people.

I find it interesting that **Enoch is the only eyewitness who wrote his chronicles in the first person ("I")** and his accounts were **interpreted by theologians unquestionably** as the words of God, **which is expected based on their faith and a religious perspective**. In Genesis it is said that Enoch walked with God for 300 years and was carried up to heaven on a fiery chariot by angels and taught their wisdom. Obviously, a **"fiery chariot"** was his way to describe a **type of vehicle that would have been impossible at that time to describe without knowledge of modern technology**.

Enoch was very much loved by his people and even though he warned them of the dangers of following him to the place of his departure, they did anyway and scores of them were **burned to death as the "fiery chariot" departed to the heavens**. His people must have believed that a **loving and all-powerful God** would do them no harm despite Enoch's warning.

The amount of **highly technical knowledge about the universe** that was imparted to Enoch was absolutely astonishing and much of what he was taught was **not known or proven to be true by researchers or scientists until thousands of years later**.

In the Book of Books in the first Book of Moses (Genesis, chapter 6 verses 1 and 2) it reads: "When men began to increase in number on the earth and daughters were born to them, the sons of God saw that the daughters of men were beautiful and they married any of them they chose." These "sons of God" were also referred to as the "fallen angels" and their number was 200 that came to earth. **How could God have "sons of God" when His only son was Jesus?**

This was **obviously at the time of Adam and Eve** because they are said to have impregnated the **daughters of Cain** as mentioned in the prior chapter. This could explain how the earth was populated with more than just Adam and Eve. This story also begs the question; were these really the sons of God, or was "God" actually a term to describe their **leader**? I say this because if this really was the "sons of God", then God must have had children that then had sex with humans. If they were "fallen angels", then it implies a falling out with an all-powerful God. **Knowing an all-powerful God first hand**, do you think that they would have disobeyed Him? **No way!**

Okay, wait, here it comes; could the only reasonable or rational explanation be that this was neither God nor the sons of God, but rather **God's earlier intelligent creation before the creation of humans, i.e. extraterrestrials**? If, in fact, these were extraterrestrials, then they would know that by disobeying their **"leader"** that they would never be allowed to return and hence earth would become their future home. This scenario would also explain their benevolence in teaching mankind in all fields of knowledge, which would help with their own survival on earth.

Keep in mind that in those ancient times it would be **absolutely impossible for humans to distinguish between technology and God**. In fact, unlike today, even **the concept or possibility of extraterrestrials was not in their conscious minds**. In other words, **there would be no way that humans at that time could distinguish between the two, absolutely no way.**

Enoch knew of the great flood because God or the "leader" told him of his plan for **revenge or retaliation** against the "sons of God" or the "fallen angels". If this was not God could it be that a great flood was the only thing that **was within the "leader's" limited power** in order to destroy those who betrayed him? **Obviously God could have destroyed whomever He wanted with the blink of an eye, right?** I speak more about the **leader's "limited power"** in

Chapter 20 and Noah and the Great Flood in the next chapter.

CHAPTER 9

NOAH AND THE GREAT FLOOD

Enoch was the father of Methuselah and the great grandfather of Noah. The Dead Sea Scrolls has a story in the Lamech scroll (**Lamech was the father of Noah**), which gives a description of Noah as being **"quite strange looking and out of place in the family"**. In fact, Lamech thought that **he looked more like the gods than men.** His wife was adamant about not having had an affair, so Lamech consulted with Enoch through his father, Methuselah, who explained that the strange looking boy had been chosen as the leader of those who would survive the flood. What flood? Well, Enoch explained that **God was very upset with His creation of man due to their wild nature and lack of adherence to any rules or laws and He regretted having created them in the first place** (Of course an all-knowing God would have known this before He created man.), **so He was planning to destroy all but the chosen ones with a Great Flood.** This begs the questions: **How can God possibly have**

regrets and what rules or laws were in place at that time, and how were they communicated to man and by whom? I attempt to provide an answer to the latter question in Chapter 16.

It is extremely interesting to note that 1,200 different cultures have ancient stories or myths about a **great flood** that encompassed the entire world.

The Great Flood is said to have covered the entire earth and there is evidence of seashells on high mountains around the world, including sea fossils in Puma Punku, Bolivia at an elevation of 13,000 feet above sea level. Other than the effects of tides, keep in mind that **"sea level" is a relative constant worldwide** so it is impossible to have the sea level rise by thousands of feet in the Mediterranean Sea and not in all of the other oceans of the world (impossible). If it was just a local flood, then they could have simply moved to higher grounds, like to Turkey's Mount Ararat with its elevation of 17,000 feet above sea level, which is said to be the location that the ark is thought to have come to rest after the waters had receded.

As the chosen one, it would then be up to Noah (with possibly his enhanced DNA from the gods) and his family to start populating the earth all over again. The ark that Noah built was probably a really large boat; however, how utterly difficult would it have been to save two of every species as we are taught in the Bible?

With our modern knowledge of DNA could it have possibly been that a DNA collection process was actually used? Also, from a pragmatic standpoint, how utterly difficult would it have been to clean up after and feed all of them, not to mention obvious safety issues for both animals and humans from natural predators. Some may demand a little more food than what Noah was "rationing" out to them, since he wouldn't have known how long they would be stuck on the Ark. **With a DNA collection the problem is completely solved with no food, safety or sanitary issues, but this obviously implies advanced scientific knowledge, but from whom?**

In any case, regardless of how it was done, "God" essentially wiped out almost all of mankind. **This begs the questions; did "God" actually make a mistake creating man in the first place?**

Since God can not make a mistake, then is it possible that an alternative answer could possibly be that these stories are either not true or that this was not about God at all, but rather about the gods as described in mythology? Also, is the killing of thousands or hundreds of thousands if not millions of people something that a "loving God" would do? Is this the same God that gave us the Ten Commandments, which included "Thou shalt not kill" and who also punished Cain for killing Abel well before His Ten Commandments?

Okay, here is another theory; is it possible that God did not create the Great Flood, which may have simply been a natural force of nature, but rather He actually saved mankind by having Noah become the caretaker of mankind and earth's creatures? Alternatively, if God was not involved and it was not a natural force of nature, then could it have been caused by the "gods" from another planet that were experimenting with the creation of humans and in the process they had made mistakes and wanted to start over again? I revisit this topic extensively in Chapter 20.

If we were to set up shop on another planet, is this something that we might do, i.e. create an ecosystem of plants etc. and then seed the planet with other forms of life including intelligent beings based on our DNA? We actually have the ability to do that right now; however, moral and governmental laws preclude us from cloning or creating test tube babies at least for now on our planet. What will we be capable of doing in the next one hundred to a thousand years from now?

Have you noticed a continual reference to "gods" as opposed to just "God" in the scriptures? The plural use of God is apparent in the Bible referring to our creation as it is stated that we were created in "their" image. Is it possible that the plural use was just a reference to the Trinity (Father, Son and Holly Spirit)? Are we then to believe that God looks just like us, or is it a spiritual image?

Okay, the Great Flood is said to have happened in the Bible, but why did God wait another 10,000 years (my estimate based on the flood being about 12,000 years ago after the end of the last ice age) after the flood before He sent Jesus to save us from our sins? It sounds like mankind could have used a heavy dose of saving prior to the Great Flood, right? And if we needed saving 10,000 years later, then we must have reverted back to the old ways of the first humans whom God wiped out in the Great Flood. As described in Chapter 7, some of the Nephilim survived the Great Flood, so evil was still on the earth as recorded in the subsequent story of **Sodom and Gomorrah**, which is discussed in the next chapter.

Since it has been 2,000 years since Jesus left us, what would God think of us now with all of the wars and killings over the years? I would surmise that He is not pleased in the least (just my opinion). Jesus said that He would return some day; so it begs the question, will it be soon enough to save us, or will it be more like the "wrath of God" whereby mankind is once again wiped out?

CHAPTER 10

SODOM AND GOMORRAH

The exact date of the destruction of the cities of Sodom and Gomorrah is unknown, however scholars estimate the destruction to be between 2070 and 1900 BC, which was at least 600 years before Moses received the Ten Commandments, so this also begs the question; what rules or laws were in place at that time and how were they communicated to man and by whom? Once again, I will attempt to propose an answer to that question in Chapter 16.

As described in the Bible, Lot and his family were **righteous people** so they were given a warning to evacuate the city and then **swiftly** escorted out of the city by "two angels" just prior to its complete destruction in "fire and brimstone", due to the evil that was rampant. Who were these benevolent angels and why did they need to "swiftly" escape the city? Well, in retrospect they needed to move swiftly, because they just barely make it out in the nick of time, but why such a close call? Why didn't God give them a little more time to get out? **Was God possibly on a strict timetable?** This makes no sense, so do you think that if this was not about God and His angels at all, but rather about the gods who had planned an air strike for a specific time like we do today, then it would make a lot more sense? Could the description in the Bible of "fire and brimstone" actually be a description in today's terms of a **nuclear bomb**? After all, wasn't Lot and his family given strict instructions to not look back at the city or else they would die? Why would they die for simply looking back? Was it for disobeying God, or was it possibly for some other reason?

Unfortunately, Lot's wife did look back and did die according to the Bible. If it was, in fact, a nuclear bomb, then is it possible that she was blinded, fell down and couldn't continue to the safety of a cave from the radioactive fallout? If this was the case, then was the warning to not look back based on not seeing God's weapons of mass destruction, but rather a warning for their own benefit to keep them from being blinded; or could it possibly have been both? Or was it possibly a test of their loyalty and obedience to God? **This would seem to be a "very strange test" because God already favored them for being "righteous people", right?**

Oh, by the way the story in the Bible of Lot's wife turning into a pillar of salt is very strange. Was it a way to explain God's power and the creation of the salty Dead Sea, as opposed to her death being from simply being blinded? Being an all-knowing God why would He allow this to happen since He would have known what was going to happen? Well, I guess one could simply say, "They were warned weren't they?" Also, 120 to 150 pounds of salt would be far from what would be required to create the salty Dead Sea.

Biblical scholars and archeologists believe that the location of the two cities (Sodom and Gomorrah) was on the south eastern shores of the Dead Sea, which was near the ancient city of Zoar where Lot found sanctuary in a cave in the hills overlooking Zoar, which is just south of the Dead Sea.

CHAPTER 11

MOSES AND THE ARK OF THE COVENANT

Then there is the story of Moses and the Ark of the Covenant, which is equally amazing with his eyewitness accounts of his encounter with God in the 13th century B.C. (1,200 to 1,300 BC). In the Book of Books (Exodus) Moses has his encounter with God, **but he never actually sees God**, but he does receive **extremely detailed instructions for building the Ark of the Covenant**. These instructions also included safety warnings regarding not making any mistakes or deviations from the design including a warning regarding the safe transportation of the Ark. In fact, Moses recorded that when Uzzah grabbed the Ark to help stabilize or save it from turning over and being damaged, **"he was killed as if struck by lightning"**. (Today this would have resulted in one hell of a wrongful death product's liability lawsuit due to a **faulty and dangerous design**.) Why would God not have designed a foolproof safety protection for those near the

Ark, and being an all-knowing God why would He allow this to happen since He would have known what was going to happen? Well, once again I guess one could simply say, "They were warned weren't they?"

The Ark of the Covenant is thought to have housed the two stone tablets of the Ten Commandments, which were given to Moses, but it is also thought to be a **communication device with God and a powerful weapon.** Why would God have wanted a communication device? Is it possible that it would allow Him to communicate with humans without being seen? (I address this interesting question further in Chapter 17.)

As to it being a powerful weapon, I seriously doubt that it was because it was built by humans using common materials at their disposal (no plutonium or uranium etc.); however, **it very well could have "appeared" to be a powerful weapon** since a signal sent to God from the Ark regarding the enemy's location could have resulted in an awe inspiring airstrike, just like it is today. They speak to God via the Ark and suddenly their enemy is vaporized, so why wouldn't it be described as a "powerful weapon" and a communication device?

The fact that Uzzah was basically "electrocuted" doesn't mean that it was from a powerful weapon since a "shock" from a high-powered communication transmission device could possibly have killed him. To the witnesses it may have appeared as if he was struck by lightning since an understanding of an electrical shock was not known at that time, so "lightning" would have been the only description that they could have possibly used. What else could they have possibly said to describe what happened? The description of his death certainly wasn't one of radiation poisoning or of an accidental ordinance explosion from some type of weapon.

It is said that God loves "us" unconditionally; however, His actions of killing our ancestors (i.e. the Great Flood, Sodom and Gomorra and Uzzah) seems to contradict this belief. Maybe it depends on the definition of "us", which could mean just believers. Or once again, maybe this wasn't the action of God but rather of the gods, right?

CHAPTER 12

TOWER OF BABEL

It is thought that in about 800 BC a united humanity built a city and tower to reach heaven. Do you think they were literally attempting to reach heaven? Do you think they could possibly have been that stupid? If they were building a tower **"towards heaven"** and not "to heaven", then it makes a lot more sense, right?

At any rate, the theme in Genesis appears to be a competition between God and the humans. God supposedly was **"concerned"** that the humans built the tower to avoid a second flood. It is interesting to note that **Sumerian myth** has a similar story to that of the Tower of Babel and an Assyrian myth dated from about 800 BC has a number of similarities to the subsequent written Biblical story.

When God observed this tower He took great offense to humans attempting to subvert His power or authority. In Genesis it is reported that the Lord said, "Indeed the people are one and they all have one language, and this is what they begin to do; now nothing that they propose to do will be withheld from them. Come, **let us** go down there and confuse their language that they may not understand one another's speech." He then scattered them around the world. Why would He say, "Come, **let us**", which would imply that God was either soliciting or commanding other's help, right? Why would God need help? Could this possibly be the action of the gods rather than an all-powerful God? Also, God would hardly need a divided or confused people in order to take any retribution of His liking would He?

How long do you think "God" thought His plan of confusing our language would last before we would overcome that obstacle and once again be united in our ability to communicate and endeavor to preserve our ability to survive disasters? Well, over the following 2,800 years to the present day, have we humans once again offended "God" by uniting ourselves with our ability to communicate between all languages very easily and very quickly? It appears as if "God's" plan of dividing us has been undermined.

Unlike our ancestors, we aren't building towers as a defense against a second flood, but we are attempting to survive any catastrophic event via our space exploration, space station and rockets to shoot down or deflect asteroids, not to mention plans of establishing colonies on the moon and/or on other planets like Mars. If God was extremely concerned about our ancestors building a simple tower, then what do you believe He thinks of us now?

Our space program, which started in the 1960's, is now well over 50 years old with our landing on the moon in 1969, so it begs the question; just like God's reaction to the Tower of Babel, why has He not interfered with our pursuit of space travel? As stated earlier, the Tower of Babel action doesn't seem likely to be the action of a "concerned" God but rather the action of the gods. So, if this was the action of the gods, then are they still observing us and why have they not taken any action against our space exploratory ambitions? Do we have anything to fear in the future from God or the gods as we make even more progress?

CHAPTER 13

EZEKIEL'S VISION

The prophet Ezekiel believed to have been born in 622 BC and is reported to have met God and had visions from 592 to 570 BC. In the Bible according to the prophet Ezekiel he talks about a "vision of God" traveling from earth to heaven and back in some type of vehicle described as having wheels within wheels with **a cloud of smoke, fire and a thunderous sound like a huge waterfall.** This is a very interesting description at a time when there was a **total lack of any possible understanding of modern technology**, but one that could very well have been the description of some sort of powered aircraft if described in today's terms.

It is hard to believe that an all-powerful God would need or even elect to travel in any type of vehicle whatsoever, so it begs the question **was this really God visiting earth as chronicled in the Bible?** Was this just a "vision" of Ezekiel in his mind's eye or was this actually something that he saw that was **misunderstood technology** of the gods?

CHAPTER 14

BIRTH OF JESUS CHRIST

Jesus Christ was born approximately 2,000 years ago (actually it was about 5 or 6 BC based on an analysis of King Herod's chronology of ordering the killing of all male babies up to 2 years old and with the date of Herod's death in 4 BC), which was almost 1,300 years after the Ten Commandments were handed down to man through Moses.

The birth of Jesus happened thousands of years (possibly tens of thousands of years) after the arrival of both the Nephilim (the fallen angels in the Bible) and the subsequent Great Flood, so Jesus was born in a totally different era after Noah (the righteous one) who with his family repopulated the world after the Great Flood, **but evil still existed after the flood**, which was the reason for Jesus's birth, i.e. to save us from our sins.

Fortunately, Mary the virgin mother of Jesus shared Noah's to Abraham's genetic history (absolutely no Nephilim genes), which is well documented in the Bible, therefore Jesus was born as 100% man and 100% God as the Savior of mankind.

Why did God specifically choose this period of time to have Jesus born? If God had waited just another 2,000 years before sending Jesus, then do you think that His message would have been more effectively communicated and received around the world? How much more effective would His message have been using TV coverage and video recordings of not only His message but also of His miracles? Based on the amount of evil present at the time of Jesus, maybe any delay would have made it impossible to save mankind in subsequent years.

The New Testament was written between 50 and 90 AD and **the copying of the Bible was extremely slow as it was painstakingly copied by hand.** Writing about events that happened a half-century or more in the past is not the most effective reporting protocol. Additionally, unlike today, both the distribution and **translation into different languages** were just other major barriers for getting the Word of God to the people. **Is it somewhat**

ironic that "God's" action at Babel actually worked against getting His Word out to the people? In fact, the mass production of the Bible did not take place until about 1,450 AD after the invention of the Gutenberg printing press. And it wasn't until 1519 AD that Cortez and his missionaries visited the Aztecs in the western hemisphere to spread the Word; so once again, doesn't it really beg the question of why such an "early birth" of Jesus, but then once again it may have been a critical tipping point in time?

Also, is it possible that God intentionally designed the conveyance of His message via the Bible to be subject to interpretation and controversy because He didn't want us to be "a doubting Thomas" but rather He wanted us to have questions but then to embrace "faith" and accept it without question as in "blind faith"? This would certainly lead to less than a unanimous or even a majority acceptance of His Word.

CHAPTER 15

CHRONOLOGY

From a chronological standpoint I find it informative to note the following events previously discussed in their respective order and time frame:

Adam and Eve: God created Adam and Eve, but one must question if this was God's first creation of man due to the stories of Cain and his fearing **"strangers"** after being exiled from the garden.

The Nephilim: The Nephilim were the offspring of the fallen angels that corrupted mankind and the reason why God regretted having created man and animals in the first place. Therefore, He decided to wipe out His creation with the Great Flood, but unfortunately some evil Nephilim survived as witnessed by the Sodom and Gomorrah story in the Bible. Did God need a better plan to kill the Nephilim?

Enoch: Enoch was taken from earth by God in a "fiery chariot" and taught by the gods in all things for the benefit of mankind.

Obviously, a "fiery chariot" was his way to describe a **type of vehicle** that would have been impossible at that time to describe without knowledge of modern technology. Enoch was very much loved by his people and even though he warned them of the dangers of following him to the place of his departure, they did and scores of them were burned to death as the "fiery chariot" departed to the heavens. His people must have believed that a **loving and all-powerful God** would do them no harm despite Enoch's warning.

The Great Flood: About 10,000 BC (my estimate) "God" was very upset with his creation of man due to their wild nature and lack of adherence to any rules or laws, so He essentially wiped out mankind. He regretted having created man, so **did He make a mistake?** This happened about 8,700 years before Moses and the Ten Commandments, so again what rules or laws were in place at that time and how was it communicated to man? As previously stated, I attempt to provide an answer to this question in the next chapter (Chapter 16).

The Destruction of Sodom and Gomorrah: The exact date is unknown, but scholars estimate the destruction to be between 2070 and 1900 BC, which was at least 600 years before Moses received the Ten Commandments, so once again what rules or laws were in place at that time and how were they communicated to man and by whom? Also, why was Lot's wife killed? **Didn't "God" favor her as being a righteous person?**

Moses and the Ark of the Covenant: Moses received the Ten Commandments in about 1,300 BC, which was about 8,700 years after the Great Flood. Why did God wait for almost nine thousand years before giving mankind a heads-up as to what was not acceptable to Him via the Ten Commandments? The next chapter attempts to answer that question.

Why did Moses never actually see God and why did God allow Uzzah to accidently die, since it was foreseeable? Was the Ark of the Covenant a communication device with God and was it also a weapon?

The Tower of Babel: About 500 years after receiving His Commandments, was mankind becoming paranoid of the possible "wrath of God" because they knew they were not obeying his Commandments and feared a second flood as a consequence? Even though God had told them that he would not have another flood, did they decide to build a tower for their own protection from rising waters in case He changed His mind?

Once again, was Babel the action of God, or of the gods? Isn't it difficult if not impossible to believe that humans were capable of competing with an all-powerful God in any way shape or form? And of course the **real God** would know that **He had absolutely nothing to be concerned about**, so without a concern then why any action at all? Also, how long do you think "God" thought His plan of confusing our language would last before we would overcome that obstacle and once again be united in our ability to communicate and endeavor to preserve our ability to survive disasters?

Ezekiel's Vision: The prophet Ezekiel believed to have been born in 622 BC and is reported to have met God and had visions from 592 to 570 BC. In the Bible according to the prophet Ezekiel he talks about a "vision of God" traveling from earth to heaven and back in some type of craft described as having wheels within wheels with **a cloud of smoke, fire and a thunderous sound like a huge waterfall.**

Birth of Jesus Christ: Jesus was born approximately 2,000 years ago (actually it was probably about 5 to 6 BC based on an analysis of King Herod's chronology of ordering the killing of all male babies up to 2 years old and with the date of his own death in 4 BC), which was almost 1,300 years after the Ten Commandments were handed down to man through Moses.

CHAPTER 16

RULES AND LAWS BEFORE THE TEN COMMANDMENTS

As you have noticed, I have often questioned what rules or laws governed man before the Ten Commandments and what rules or laws were in place at that time and how were they communicated to man and by whom. Well, I feel it only proper to venture a theory based on what others have proposed as an answer.

Since sin existed from the time of Adam, the word "sin" implies a violation of a rule or law well before Moses and the Ten Commandments, right? Consequently, God's law must have existed even though it was not written down. Remember that it is said that both Adam and Eve were given specific **verbal commands from God**.

God gave us both a **conscience and free will**, which has an **implied understanding of a sense of what is right or wrong**. Essentially, it is **a choice between good and evil. Our**

conscience has a natural sense of right and wrong, so every normal or sane person has not only a basic concept of right and wrong, but also of love and selfishness.

Taking another's life or murder is something that I believe even an atheist understands is against a moral law. Cain knew that it was wrong to kill Abel as **he was greatly troubled by it**, which was dictated by his **guilty conscience**. **This is innate in all humans even if it is not written down.**

Before leaving this subject matter, I find it interesting that incest, which is strictly forbidden today, must have been acceptable at the time of Adam and Eve. How else could just two people begin to populate the world? However, if in fact there were other humans at that time and Adam and Eve were not God's first creation, then incest may not have happened nor have been acceptable. And as we know today, incest produces genetically defective beings, so just another great reason to ban it. Can you imagine how defective all humans would have been after just a few generations of incestuous breeding.

CHAPTER 17

THE FACE OF GOD

One thing that I find very strange is that **"God" never wanted anyone to see Him** (including Moses) but to only to hear His voice, which may have been the reason for the Ark of the Covenant to be **a communication devise. The stated reason was that He is such a brilliant vision, brighter than the sun; that we would, as a matter of fact, be killed if we saw His face.** I don't know about you, but my God would have been able to show us His face if He wanted without killing us. Could there be another explanation? Is it possible that if we saw "His" face that we would not die but rather "He" would have something to lose? Could it be possible that, if this was not God, but rather the gods (astronauts), they didn't want humans to see that they needed breathing masks and spacesuits to live in our atmosphere, which would obviously expose them as being less like Gods and more like mortal beings?

I would like for you to consider a hypothetical question; if when we landed on the moon in 1969 we had found an intelligent life form similar to our own but who were over 200,000 years behind our intellectual and technological development, i.e. pre homo sapien, then would this intelligent life form view our astronauts as supernatural beings or "Gods" just like we might have done in our past? If these moon people only heard our voices and never saw us, then they would not have questions about our need for spacesuits, right? The spacesuits would clearly expose us to being less than Gods; however, we would obviously need to make up a reason for why these moon people would not be allowed to see us in our spacesuits if we wanted them to think of us as Gods. But why would we want to be thought of as all-powerful Gods? Well, possibly for our own protection from an uprising or any attempt to challenge our authority as we exploit the moon's natural resources.

We may even want to encourage leadership amongst the inhabitance in the form of **kingships or religions** in order to exercise control over an ignorant populous through their leaders who have curried favor with us. We might even teach them in ways to make their lives better as a sign of our benevolence. And to further this line of thinking, suppose that Russia and China decided to compete for the moon's natural resources, then that would certainly lead to conflicts from time to time. The moon people would obviously side with the ones who were the most benevolent and who protected them from any collateral damage from the weapons of the "evil ones". Our enemies are always the "evil ones", i.e. "Axis of Evil".

Additionally, if these moon people were too stupid to be of any use to us, then we may want to share our DNA to make a more intelligent being. If this were to happen, then with our DNA would these beings have a soul? Taking this hypothetical question full circle we must ask ourselves the question; namely, **if ancient astronauts via their DNA created us, then do we have a soul?** In other words, do subsequent secondhand creations of intelligent beings with the DNA of God's first creation have the "soul gene" in it? **I believe that anyone with a conscience with free will and the inherit ability to distinguish between right and wrong would have a God given soul.** I speak more on this topic in Chapter 22 and in the Epilogue.

Lastly, if after we left the moon would these moon people continue to evolve into smarter and smarter people? If so, would they some day question their existence and through scientific analysis question their evolutionary leap to more intelligent beings and hence contemplate their own "missing link"? **They may even ponder the existence of a God**. Their quest for the missing link would end up being no more successful than ours because we would be long gone; however, from time to time we may want to observe their progress from afar, which they may actually refer to as UFO sightings.

CHAPTER 18

THE CREATION OF THE UNIVERSE

If we want to gain more knowledge, we need to go back to the beginning of time. Scientists estimate that the creation of the universe began with what is commonly referred to as the "Big Bang", which is thought to have occurred about 9 billion years ago and with our earth being formed about 4.5 billion years ago. Have you ever wondered what happened before 9 billion years ago? I guess that the answer to this question is as difficult as understanding the concept of infinity. Greek astronomers debated whether the universe was finite or infinite and the conundrum was that, **"If you reached your hand through the edge of the boundary of the universe, then where would your hand be?"**

How could the Big Bang have been created from nothing? Since something can't come from nothing, there must have been intelligence behind it. This alone should give one reason to believe in a Creator or a God.

Most have heard of the "Goldilocks zone"(not too hot and not too cold), which scientists use to refer to a critical zone away from our Sun that can support life. If the earth were closer to the Sun, then the oceans would have evaporated and had earth been further away then the oceans would have frozen. Either way we would not have had life, as we know it. Relative to time, as we know it, one could assume that God was in no hurry to create us. If fact, assuming there is a God, why did He create dinosaurs first well over 250 million years before man? And why did He wipe out the dinosaurs 65 million years ago with an **asteroid**? Was this a mistake or some type of a master plan?

Mammals survived the asteroid with the more intelligent forms being called primates from which some people believe we evolved. Why "evolve" since He could have created anything that He wished, including a fully evolved human species from the get-go without a long evolutionary process? Is it possible that He did create intelligent beings millions of years ago but on a different planet or possibly on earth millions of years ago with no trace left of their existence?

Is it possible that these earlier intelligent beings decided to explore space as we are doing today and found a more suitable planet in which to inhabit? Is it also possible that nuclear war broke out in antiquity and our great ancestors essentially destroyed our ability to live on earth for thousands of years due to radioactive fallout from a nuclear bomb? And is it possible that these intelligent ancestors came back to earth 200,000 years ago or more to inhabit or possibly genetically alter life on our planet? **Could their DNA be the "missing link" in the creation or evolution of man?** They would have been much more advanced than we are today and it has been proven that we now have the ability to alter DNA and play God ourselves.

There are many who believe that we evolved from the apes or chimpanzees; however, scientists have found that they share 97% to 98% of the same DNA as humans, which is very compelling, but the 2% to 3% difference is too significant to have evolved without a "missing link" that is still a mystery. Evolution may be possible but not from apes or chimpanzees (impossible) and humans do not share enough DNA with Neanderthals, so if we evolved whom did we evolve from?

Researchers in 2017 have found no trace of Neanderthal Y-chromosomes in modern man. The fact that modern humans have some Neanderthal DNA means that humans may have interbred with Neanderthals (but probably only after a few beers). **The so-called "missing link" in the theory of evolution would be required to connect all of the dots, but it will never be discovered, as it is a tremendously flawed theory.** The genesis of evolution of animals has been proven and is very interesting and absolutely compelling; however, to apply that theory to humans may sound very logical, but with our ever-increasing scientific knowledge, i.e. DNA, it is **absolutely impossible.**

CHAPTER 19

THE EVIDENCE OR MYSTERIES

Even with so many modern day sightings of UFO's with some incredible stories by very credible pilots that are difficult to debunk, I will not be addressing these as there are way too many and there is no physical proof even though some of the sightings appeared on radar or sketchy video. Instead, my search for knowledge will focus on evidence in the form of **ancient scriptures, unexplained mysterious structures and other ancient artifacts** that we can actually see and touch here on earth; therefore, I have included a number of pictures because we all know how many words a picture is worth.

It is my understanding that modern archeologists have excluded a number of artifacts that are very strange and do not fit the accepted narrative of our ancient civilizations. These artifacts have actually been removed from public displays in museums and are buried in back room storage lockers.

From my reading it appears that there were a number of belief systems based on encounters with mystical beings that were referred to as gods, which then escalated into a competition of sorts, which was reflected in numerous stories of aerial battles especially in India's Hindu Sanskrit texts 15,000 years ago that chronicled aerial battles in flying machines called Vimana (**Fig.1** shows what they may have looked like based on these texts). It was said that these

Fig. 1
India's Vimanas

Vimana were operated by the gods of India and were constructed with 16 different metals of which only 3 are available on earth. **The Vimana with its weapons of mass destruction is mentioned at least 40 times in the Hindu texts**. In fact, the texts chronicle a major aerial battle about 5,000 years ago that was ended when the god Krishna used what could only be described today as a nuclear weapon with its brightness a thousand times brighter than the sun, which totally wiped out two cities.

Russia is the largest country on earth with approximately 50% uninhabited and unexplored. In 1987 an archeologist research team discovered an ancient site dating from the 17th to 20th century BC in Arkaim, Russia. This site is similar to England's Stonehenge and is said to be able to measure precise features of 18 astronomical events. In 1991 geologists looking for gold found unbelievable artifacts about 600 miles north of Arkaim in the Euro mountains (between Europe and Asia). At a depth of between 10 and 40 feet, under thousands of years of undisturbed soil, they found a number of small metal fragments, which when examined under a microscope were measured as small as **1/10,000 of an inch and revealed to be coils made from tungsten, a very rare metal (Fig. 2)**. Based on the depth of these coils, they have been dated to range between 20,000 and 100,000 years old. These could have only been made by a manufacturing technology used in modern day spacecraft and the only way they

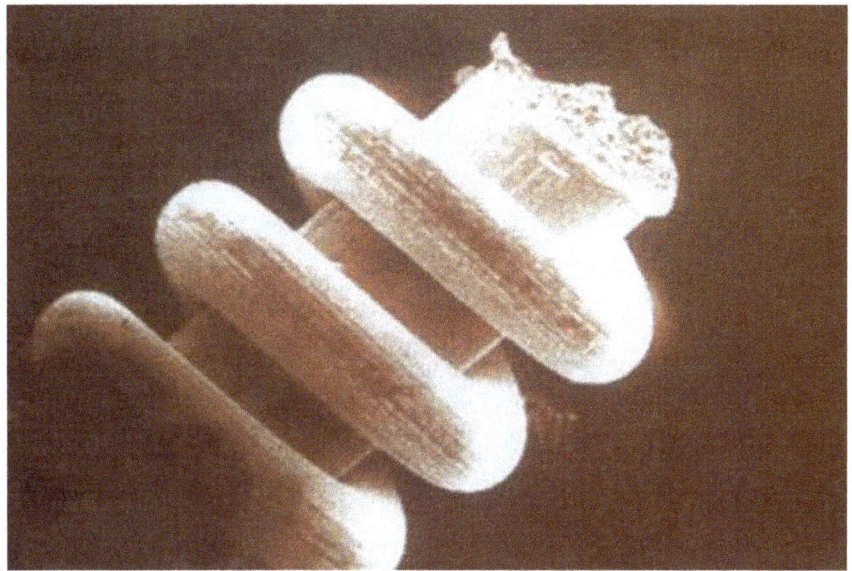

Fig. 2
1/10,000 in. magnified coil in Russia

could be produced today is with machine-guided technology (CNC machines) and not by hand (absolutely impossible). This is the technology that is also used today to manufacture semi conductors and micro computer chips that are used in circuit boards that measure a great deal less than 1/10,000 of an inch. **The speculation is that these coil fragments were from an aircraft that had crashed tens of thousands of years ago.**

What is up with the Egyptian drawings of gods with animal heads **(Fig. 3)**? What do you think was the artist's inspiration for these drawings? Was it from a creative imagination or from something that they actually saw? This is just one example of many of their blending of human and animal forms together.

Fig. 3
Egyptian God

As far as the controversy goes regarding who built the Egyptian pyramids, I am sure that you have already heard enough about those speculations, so I will move on to other less known controversies, but I must say that they were not built by man or at the very least not without "outside help".

Life on other planets would most definitely have a totally different mixture of air or gasses that make up their atmosphere, which is 100% obvious from our scientific analysis. None of the other planets that we know of have the same oxygen rich air as on earth. In fact, since hydrogen is many times more plentiful than oxygen in the universe, other intelligent life forms may require hydrogen rather than oxygen to sustain their life. Many ancient cave drawings, rock drawings and sculptures around the world show what looks like **space suits with full head helmets like (Fig. 4A, B & C)**, which are Mayan carvings that look just like a modern day astronaut. In fact, one stone carving shows what looks like a **modern day astronaut** (Maya King Pakal) in a shuttle capsule with all of its controls **(Fig. 5)**. What else could it possibly be? How strange is that? There are two theories; the first is that he was ascending to the heavens and the second is that he was descending into the underworld. Regardless of which direction he was going, isn't it strange that a vehicle was depicted? Why a vehicle and why not just a depiction of wings on his body or anything other than a vehicle? Is it possible that they were depicting something that they had actually seen in the past?

Fig. 4A
Mayan Sculpture with Helmet

Who Is the Real God?

Fig. 4B
Mayan Astronaut Carving

Fig. 4C
Mayan Sculpture with Space Suit

Fig. 5
Mayan Carving of King Pakal

Life forms from other planets would most definitely need space suits due to the difference in air and temperature between planets, just like we needed in order to land on the moon. On a beautiful 75-degree day on earth a life form from another planet may very well die of either the excessive heat or the excessive cold relative to their own climate conditions where they thrive (**Fig. 6A** shows what looks to be **a spacesuit helmet** on an Australian rock drawing). Similar rock drawing can be found in many places around the world, like in Utah, North America **(Fig. 6B)**.

Fig. 6A
Australian Rock Drawing of Spacesuit Helmet

Fig. 6B
Utah Rock Drawing of Spacesuits

As to ancient artifacts, take for example two findings, one in Egypt and one in Columbia. In an Egyptian tomb archeologists found what initially appeared to be a small wood bird carving, but was later reexamined and found to have a vertical rudder **unlike any bird in nature (Fig. 7)**. This could not have been seen and copied from nature because birds do not have vertical rudders, so where did the artist that carved this get his inspiration? Upon further examination by scientists it was determined that **the wings were designed for lift**, just like modern day planes (curved from front to back and also tapered from front to back). Upon further analysis it was determined that it was a **highly developed aerodynamic glider**.

Fig. 7
Egypt's Saqqara "Bird" with Vertical Tail

Additionally, in a Columbian burial site from pre-Columbia 1,500 years ago a **small gold "airplane" figurine** was found, which also had a **vertical tail or rudder (Fig. 8)**. It had triangular swept back wings like a fighter jet, an upright tail fin, stabilizers and a fuselage. An aviation expert made a scale model from wood, which he flew and said that it was the **perfect shape for flying**. These are two examples from across the world, which begs the question; did these people know each other, know how to fly or see these in the skies?

Fig. 8
Colombian Figurine with Vertical Tail

There are virtually hundreds of additional unexplained artifacts around the world; however, one of my favorites is the **Antikythera device (Fig. 9)**, which was about the size of a shoebox and was found in the Mediterranean Sea off the coast of the Greek island of Antikythera. Sponge divers recovered this devise from the sea in 1900 and didn't know what to make of it until it was x-rayed decades later. Then with the advent of 3-DX-rays it showed it was a **highly sophisticated astronomical devise**, which was dated to about 150 BC. It had at least 30 inter meshing bronze gears and 37 gear wheels enabling it to follow the movements of the moon and sun and predict eclipses.

Additionally, the common belief at that time in history was that all celestial bodies orbited in perfect circles; however, this devise actually tracked the irregular orbit of the moon. **So over 2,000 years ago they had the knowledge of the stars and planets along with the skill to manufacture this impressive devise, which rivals if not exceeds the workings of a Swiss watch.** It has been called an ancient celestial calculator, which was about 1,300 years ahead of its time in both knowledge and workmanship. Strangely enough this knowledge was totally lost until the 14th century European astronomical clocks.

Fig. 9
Antikythera Device

When any civilization builds, creates or accomplishes something great it is natural for them to take full credit and essentially demand respect and acknowledgment for their success from others, even if it happened thousands of years ago, like the Egyptians taking full credit for building the great pyramids of Egypt (yeah, right). This is a matter of national pride and is to be expected; however, it was surprising to learn that many ancient civilizations around the world from India to Bolivia have actually recorded that they **did not** create or build incredible structures, which anyone would have been extremely proud to claim credit. Instead they credit much earlier unknown civilizations, possibly thousands of years earlier that had builders with unbelievably superior skills than their own builders. Are we to believe that the human race's building abilities deteriorated over millennia? Does this make any sense based on our recorded history of constant innovations and advancement in our technological scientific knowledge?

Fig. 10
Temple of Jupiter in Baalbek, Lebanon

In fact, many of these structures defy belief and would be extremely difficult if not impossible to replicate even today with our superior tools and equipment, like laser cutters, diamond tip blades and mega ton cranes. Take for example the Temple of Jupiter with its **mega block platform in Baalbek, Lebanon (Fig. 10)** built about **11,000 years ago (9,000 BC)** with some blocks weighing **2,000,000 pounds** (1,000 tons). Moving two million pound quarried blocks certainly defies belief. In fact, one quarried block weighed an estimated 2.4 million pounds (2,400,000 pounds

Fig. 11A
Quarried Block in Baalbek, Lebanon

or 1,200 tons) **(Fig. 11A)**. Why would they use impossibly large blocks when they could have used blocks weighing just 2,000 pounds? **Why would they make it so difficult or incredibly hard to build these ancient structures?** The only answer that makes any sense is that it was not difficult. So it begs the question of why? It has been estimated to take 40,000 people to lift one of these massive blocks, but how could you possibly fit 40,000 people around a block that measures 62 feet long and 12 feet wide? By my calculations it would only allow space for about 74 people standing shoulder to shoulder down both sides and across both ends (62+62+12+12=148, which when divided by 2 feet for each person would give us room for just 74 people). Even using 100 people to be generous, each person would still be required to lift an astounding 20,000 pounds. If this were not difficult enough, then they would also have to transport and **lift it vertically up to 30 feet** and place it in position on top of other blocks that would fit perfectly together. Please take another look at Fig. 10 that shows two men standing on top of the foundation blocks which gives you a clear perspective of the true size of these massive blocks.

When it was originally constructed **it was constructed as a platform** and not a temple and only became a temple when the Romans conquered that area and built the Temple of Jupiter on top of the pre-existing platform in about 300 BC. The original purpose for the site is unknown, however, some have speculated that it was a **spaceport for launching and landing rockets in antiquity** (I made reference to this in **Chapter 4 regarding Gilgamesh**). If true this would certainly explain the heavy-duty foundation that would be required to support not only the rocket, but also the massive amount of thrust at lift off. As an example, at Cape Canaveral, Florida our launch pad is designed to hold well over 15,000,000-pounds of force. It accommodates a 132,000-pound rocket including fuel and payload, a 47,000-pound tower structure, a 6,000,000-pound vertical rocket transporter (crawler), a 1,400,000-pound flame deflector that slides on rails under the launch pedestal and an engine thrust of 7,800,000-pounds.

Baalbek's monumental structure must have had a very important purpose to justify its colossal construction, but what was it and how did they possibly build it in antiquity? As an engineer I have never seen a structure that did not have an intended purpose, especially one of such great magnitude. This statement also applies to the Great Pyramids of Egypt, since no one really knows the intent or real purpose behind those amazing structures (No, they were **not** tombs).

Similar mega blocks, albeit somewhat smaller, were used to build the wall at the Temple Mount in Jerusalem **(Fig. 11B)**.

Who Is the Real God?

Fig. 11B
Temple Mount in Jerusalem

Abydos, Egypt has a partially underwater temple structure that has **irregular sized blocks of stone fitted perfectly together without the use of mortar**. These were not simple rectangular blocks either, but rather irregular shaped stones with **"L" shaped blocks at the corners** with a 90-degree angle **(Fig. 12)**. You will see later in this chapter that this was not totally unique as a similar structure also appears but **on the other side of the world**.

Fig. 12
Temple Structure in Abydos, Egypt with "L" Corners

In Cusco and Machu Picchu, Peru there are **block walls fitted together so perfectly and without the use of mortar that a razor blade or paper cannot be placed between them**. And some of

Who Is the Real God?

Fig. 13A
Megalithic Structure in Peru

Fig. 13B
Megalithic Structure in Peru

Fig. 13C
Megalithic Structure in Peru

the blocks have as many as **13 angles or sides**, yet they are fitted together with other irregular blocks perfectly to form a mosaic puzzle **(Fig.**

13A, 13B & 13C). It was as if they were molded and shaped in clay and then hardened into stone. From an engineering and construction perspective, these construction designs defy belief, as one could hardly construct a wall in a more difficult manner with a **complete lack of standardization** and with multiple and exacting cuts that have **no practical purpose. It was as if they were trying to show off. As an engineer, I would be hard pressed to come up with a more difficult design**, so I must default to my standard conclusion, and that of course is that it must not have been difficult, but why?

Fig. 14
Keystone Cuts in Peru

Despite some of these blocks being huge and virtually indestructible, they were joined together using **keystone cuts and molten metal fasteners (Fig. 14)**, which further guaranteed their longevity even with massive earthquakes. These techniques also appear in Chetzuwana, Peru. And the huge megalith block wall at Ollantaytambo, Peru **(Fig. 15)** defies belief, which also used **molten metal fasteners**. All of these stone structures were built without mortar and fit together perfectly making them built to last for thousands of years. Based on the age of these structures, the pouring of molten metal was well before this technology was known to exist.

Fig. 15
Ollantaytambo, Peru

Fig. 16
"H" Block in Puma Punku, Bolivia

And then there are the incredible ruins at Puma Punku, Bolivia, which is part of Tiahuanaco **(Fig. 16)**. Modern day stonemasons have said that replicating those "H" structures would be almost impossible even with today's technology. Some of the stones weigh up to 160,000 pounds (80 tons) and the cutting of the stones were not only complex but also with these stones being diorite **(one of the hardest of all granites)** it would have required either **diamond cutting tips or laser cutting tools**, not to mention the years of training required to acquire their masonry skills. Without modern tools it would have been an impossible undertaking, so once again it must not have been difficult or they would not have succeeded, so how did they do it? **It certainly defies belief and what could possibly have been the purpose of these structures?** The Inca would have been very proud to take credit for these structures, but **they deny building them** and actually give credit to a civilization that predates them by thousands of years. In fact, based on oral records they credit the gods for building them in a single night. Wow, **oral records** just like in the Old Testament.

Despite being almost indestructible megalithic stone structures built to withstand earthquakes of great magnitude, many of these structures were nonetheless destroyed. As an example, the Puma Punku structures were completely destroyed, hence the word "ruins" of Puma Punku. At an elevation of about 13,000 feet above sea level it was interesting to note that the stone remnants were buried under about 12 feet of mud. It is speculated that it may have been the result of a great flood with all of its unbelievable force of nature. Could it have been the Great Flood as referred to in the Bible?

The Great Flood is said to have covered the entire earth and there is evidence of seashells on high elevation mountains around the world, including sea fossils found at Puma Punku. Keep in mind that other than the effect of tides "sea level" is a constant level worldwide so it is impossible to have the sea level rise in the Mediterranean Sea by thousands of feet and not in all of the other oceans of the world (impossible). If all of the mountain peaks were covered by water in Turkey (Turkey's Mount Ararat's elevation is 17,000 feet above sea level and the location that the ark is thought to have come to rest after the waters had receded), then the Puma Punku site at 13,000 feet would have been inundated as well and under a minimum of 4,000 feet of water. If the Great Flood is what actually destroyed Puma Punku about 12,000 years ago per my estimate, then that structure must have obviously existed prior to the flood, which would date the site to over 12,000 years old.

Then there are the Olmec colossal heads sculpted from basalt boulders in Mesoamerica (South America). These massive heads of which 17 have been discovered are estimated to weigh upwards of **50 tons** and were transported over long distances from the quarry. They are estimated to have been made over 3,000 years ago and have distinctive Negroid features with broad noses and full lips **(Fig. 17)**, which beg the question; did the Olmec come to South America from Africa over 3,000 years ago? If so, then how did they get there? **One might think that primitive people would be spending their time looking for food and shelter in order to survive instead of spending their days transporting and chiseling away at extremely hard granite boulders.** Once again, maybe somehow it wasn't difficult, or possibly they either weren't primitive people at all or had help from "others" more technologically advanced.

Fig. 17
Olmec Sculpture, South America

Unfortunately, it is impossible to carbon date stone, so there is no way to date these stone works by examining the stone itself. In the case of Stonehenge in England, the dating of the stone structure was estimated by the carbon dating of organic materials at the site including remnants of wood posts that were erected in antiquity that are assumed to be part of the original stone site. In the absence of provable associated materials that can be carbon dated, experts have conceded that some of these stone structures around the world could be thousands of years older than currently assumed. In fact, when it comes to dating stone structures, **they could be tens of thousands of years older than currently assumed**, but the bottom line is that we simply don't know.

At any rate, one cannot deny the number of massive stone structures around the world from Jerusalem, Iran, Spain, Lebanon, Bolivia, Peru, Greece, Chile, and Mexico etc. **Ancient legends and mythology speak of levitation** via sound waves used in floating large stone blocks in the construction of the Pyramids in Egypt, Stonehenge in England and also the mysterious stone structures in Puma Punku, Bolivia. Fifth century BC Herodias traveled to

Egypt and reported that the **Egyptians were given information from the skies of how to float large blocks into place.**

Around the world there are structures (stone wall construction) that are not just similar but have identical architecture, as if built by the same people. As one of many examples, compare the pyramids of Kong Siem Reap, Cambodia (built approximately 1,000 AD) to the pyramid of Tikal, Guatemala (built approximately 800 AD) with almost identical structures (basically pyramids with stairs to an enclosed room at the top) and are **located on separate continents (Fig. 18A & 18B)**.

Fig. 18A
Pyramid at Kong Siem Reap, Cambodia

Fig. 18B
Pyramid of Tikal, Guatemala

Also around the world there are hundreds of tall megalithic structures, all of which were built by motivated primitive people (20 to 100 ton stone blocks with similar if not identical structures). No doubt they were primitive, but I also said that they were motivated, which they must have been to undertake such a difficult task, but it begs the question; why were they motivated to undertake such a colossal project of such difficulty, unless somehow it wasn't? Some may say that it was done with slave labor, but most experts have abandoned that line of thinking. Compare the obelisk in Chauvin De Huantar, Peru to those in Egypt. Did this happen by coincidence or was there a common designer **(Fig. 19A & 19B)**? If so, how did they communicate?

Fig. 19A
Obelisk at Chauvin De Huantar, Peru

Fig. 19B
Obelisk in Egypt

The Coricancha Temple of the Sun in Cusco, Peru with their perfectly fitted stone blocks rival today's advanced machining **(Fig. 20)** and is almost identical to that of the Valley Temple in

Fig. 20
Coricancha Temple in Cusco, Peru with "L" Corners

Egypt. These were not simple rectangular blocks either, but **rather irregular shaped stones with "L" shaped blocks at the corners** with a 90-degree angle, **just like we saw in Egypt** (Please refer back to Fig. 12). These blocks were not standardized with none being the same. Once again, **without standardization there would**

be a total lack of building efficiency, as all of the blocks would be one of a kind **customized blocks**. We are talking about **200 ton blocks that were individually shaped and stacked as high as 40 feet above the ground**. If that wasn't hard enough they even make it harder as many structures were **built on impractical mountain hillsides**, like in Machu Picchu, Peru and Santorin, Greece. Once again, it must not have been difficult otherwise they would not have succeeded. They were also built without mortar as they fit together perfectly making them built to last for thousands of years. And they were almost earthquake proof by joining the blocks together by **pouring molten metal into keyways cut into the stone blocks**. As stated previously, based on the age of these structures, the pouring of molten metal was well before this technology was known to exist. This joining technique is found in Egypt, Greece, Italy, India, Cambodia, Peru, and in Tewanaku and Puma Punku, Bolivia. Could this be even more evidence of a common designer or at least corroboration?

Some of these huge rocks that were fitted together like a jigsaw puzzle showed signs of extreme heating, or what is called "vitrafication", a melting of the rock supposedly to facilitate the fitting together perfectly without gaps and no need for mortar. Obviously this would have been impossible, but then again it appears that nothing was impossible for our ancient relatives does it?

Modern science has actually proven without a doubt that **levitation is possible using sound waves**, albeit with very light objects; but it is nonetheless possible. This research is in its infancy, so given time possibly this mystery will be eventually solved. Then there is the story in the Bible of the destruction of the **walls of Jericho** using sound from horns and marching in a harmonic cadence. If it is to be believed, is it possible that sound waves were very much understood well beyond our understanding today?

Other than the incredible Egyptian pyramids their most amazing achievements to me are the incredible faces **on the Egyptian giant stone statues with their precision symmetry (Fig. 21)**. Modern day sculptures never create the "perfect" facial symmetry of the Egyptians, nor do they care because it is not detectible by the human eye and quite frankly, the human face is never perfectly symmetrical in real life anyway. The Egyptians created the faces of their statues to near perfection from not only side to side but from one statue to the next. We are talking about tolerances of plus or minus one hundredth of an inch or less and most are **absolutely perfect**. It is as if they were mass-produced from a production mold. How could they have possibly accomplished this, especially at that point in time with their limited tools and without the use of today's laser measuring photographic aids?

Fig. 21
Precision Symmetry of Egyptian Statues

Sixth century BC Pythagoras traveled through Egypt for at least a decade and received information far ahead of its time regarding sound, mathematics and music, which he said is in harmony with the universe. Pythagoras's "Music of the spheres" concluded that each planet emits sound with a specific frequency unique to that planet. This has then led to **"String Theory"**. As smart as he was considered to be, there is absolutely no way that he could have come up with this on his own **(no way)**.

I was surprised to learn that **Goebekli Tepe, Turkey** is the site of an ancient temple or structure that is dated to more than 11,000 years ago which was built by "hunter gatherers". Incredibly it predated Stonehenge by 6,000 years and the first Egyptian pyramids by 5,000 years. The structure consists of a large number of carvings from limestone in "T" shapes up to 18 feet in height with detailed carvings of a number of wild animals **(Fig. 22)**. In August 2017 information was released from scientists in Turkey after they had successfully deciphered the carvings on these stone pillars and they are telling us that **the inhabitants were leaving a**

Fig. 22
"T" Pillar in Gobekli Tepe, Turkey

message of a comet that struck earth about 13,000 years ago, which caused massive flooding and great destruction. Based on this information it is believed that the site was an **ancient observatory.** Since only 5% of the site has been excavated, I am sure that there will be exciting updates in the near future, so stay tuned.

And then there are the pinecone "devices" that appear in many depictions of ancient Egyptian art **(Fig. 23)**, which often show Assyrian Deities (gods) with pinecones prominently displayed in their hands. (Did you also notice the nice "wrist watch", which begs the question; what is it and what is its purpose?) The largest pinecone

Fig. 23
Assyrian God in Egypt

Statue in the world is in the Vatican **(Fig. 24)**. Even the Pope's staff **(Fig. 25A)** has a pinecone as does the staff of Bacchus **(Fig. 25B)**. If that was not intriguing enough the pinecone also appears on the staff of Osiris **(FIG. 26A)** and Dionysus **(Fig. 26B)**.

Fig. 24
Vatican Statue

Fig. 25A
Pope's Staff

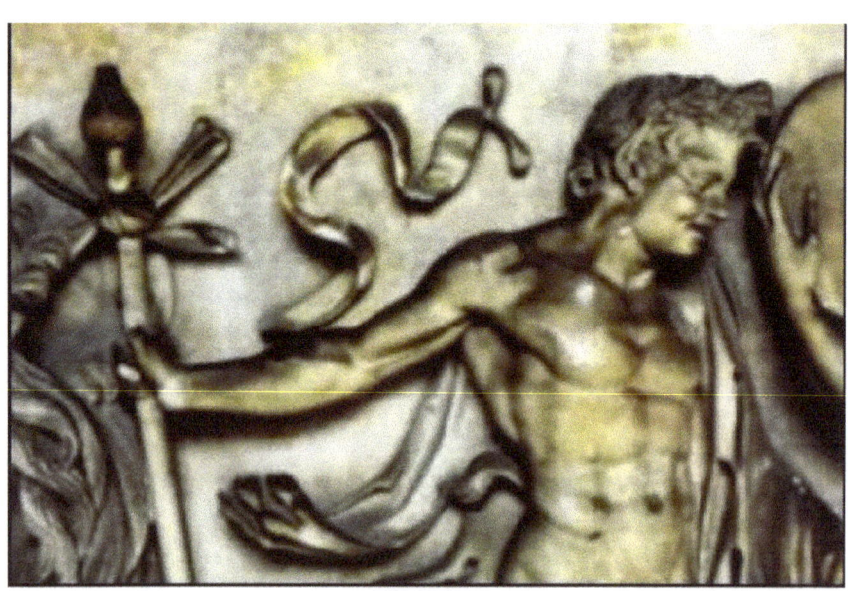

Fig. 25B
Staff of Bacchus

Who Is the Real God?

Fig. 26A
Staff of Osiris

Fig. 26B
Staff of Dionysus

Does this pinecone symbolize something? If it was just a symbol then I could understand the statue and staffs being a symbol of something, but the depiction of it in the **hand of the Assyrian Deity** implies to me that it was more than just a philosophical symbol, but rather an **actual device**. It obviously must be something of importance or it would not be so ubiquitous and is the subject of much discussion and debate. Could it be a weapon, levitation tool or communication device? In any event it must have been of great value as it is associated with kings, rulers and gods in antiquity.

If we had a time machine today that would allow us to take some of our technology of today back five thousand years, then how would our ubiquitous cell phones be depicted in their art (drawings and or statues)? Most likely it would be viewed as a magical communication device of the ruling class or gods. Can you imagine how impressed our ancient ancestors would be with this miraculous communication device in the hands of their leaders? It certainly would be something that they would associate with their leaders or gods in their depictions or art.

A number of historians believe that the pinecone is simply a symbol of the highest degree of spiritual illumination or the awakening of the "Third Eye", which is the eye of the mind, soul and reason.

Is it possible that there were ancient civilizations hundreds of thousands or millions of years ago that were highly advanced in science and technology to the point of being superior to our current level of development? If so, then where is the physical proof? Other than the stone structures already described, almost any other type of structure would have certainly decayed over hundreds of thousands or millions of years including our modern day buildings. **Stone is the only material that would survive the test of time**; therefore, that is all that is remaining today and unfortunately stone cannot be carbon dated to determine its age.

CHAPTER 20

ANALYSIS, SPECULATIONS & CONCLUSIONS

As previously stated, I believe that it takes an infinite amount of faith to believe that there is no God than to believe that there is a God; therefore, my basic premise is that there is a God, but who is He? Also, as previously stated, I make a number of factual statements; however, **please do not overlook the fact that there are at least 150 question marks (?)**, which are not statements of facts but rather provocative statements of what may or may not be fact based. I leave it up to the reader to decide what to embrace and what to discard as unreasonable. The same is true with what you are about to read.

Even though Einstein was skeptical of religious beliefs as told in the Bible, he is quoted as having said, "Everyone who is seriously involved in the pursuit of science becomes convinced that a spirit is manifest in the laws of the universe-a Spirit vastly superior to that of man." I too am skeptical of Biblical stories and have also concluded, as Einstein did, that the more we learn about the mathematical laws of the universe the more that my belief in a God is reinforced.

Were there any humans on earth prior to God's creation of Adam and Eve? It appears from the scriptures that there must have been other humans or beings when looking at Caine's life after his exile. So who were these people? Were they possibly God's earlier creation before humans?

In the Old Testament in the Bible it speaks of the Nephilim who were described as the offspring of the "fallen angels" who had sexual relations with human women. It was also said that these fallen angels had descended to earth from the heavens (skies) and were described as giant men and the "sons of God". Could these fallen angels have been the "gods" as viewed by humans that were recorded in mythology and in ancient scriptures?

How does one explain the megalithic stone structures around the world without questioning the possibility of "outside help" from another superior intelligent life form in our distant past?

Is it easier for you to believe that primitive man built these structures or to believe that superior beings of unknown origin built them? As an engineer, these structures are the **most compelling physical evidence of "outside help".** These structures alone should at least give us reason to believe that something extremely strange happened in the past around the world that we do not yet fully understand. Certainly we must admit that our history or pre-history is very strange with no black or white answers

Another interesting observation is that "God", through His actions as described in the Bible, was not perfect; **He made mistakes.** Say what? Take for example the creation and then destruction of man by the Great Flood. Enoch explained that **God was very upset with His creation of man due to their wild nature and lack of adherence to any rules or laws and He regretted having created them in the first place** (Of course an all-knowing God would have known this before He created man), **so He was planning to destroy all but the chosen ones with a Great Flood.** Do you think that an all-powerful God could have simply eliminated whomever He wanted with the blink of an eye? And according to the Bible the Great Flood didn't succeed in killing all of the evil Nephilim, so once again was this just another failure of "God"? **Therefore, could this have actually been the action of a fallible so-called god and not of an infallible God, i.e. our ancient ancestors or extraterrestrial astronauts that were God's earlier intelligent creations prior to humans?**

If the Great Flood was the action of the gods and not of God, then how could they possibly have created this massive flood with their limited powers (obviously they were not as powerful as God)? One speculation is that just like we now have the ability to redirect a large asteroid away from earth using missiles, the gods would have been able to redirect asteroids toward earth. A number of large asteroids hitting our oceans around the world could have caused massive tsunamis that would have been able to **wash over** mountains at an elevation of 29,000 feet, which is the height of Mount Everest (Mount Ararat is at an elevation of 17,000 feet, which is where the Ark is thought to have landed after the water receded).

"Washing over" the mountains makes a lot more sense because if the sea levels actually rose to the tops of the mountains around the world, then where would all of that water subsequently drain off to in order for the water levels to recede as we are told in the Bible? The earth would become **100% under water forever**, or until underwater volcanoes created new landmasses, which would be an extremely slow process over millions of years. Our current sea level around the world is a great drainage point for rain and floods on land, but if the sea level is higher than the land, then there would be absolutely nowhere for the water to drain. The amount of water to elevate **just the oceans (excluding land)** to a height of 29,000 feet would require an additional volume of water of **211%** greater than all of the waters in the oceans, and **this doesn't even include the amount of water needed to cover the land**. The average depth of the oceans is 13,740 feet, so the oceans alone would have to increase by another 29,000 feet, which is a **211%** increase (29,000/13,740 = **211%**). A globe of water at 29,000 feet is obviously not possible, so that discussion ends here.

Since the Great Flood only needed to cover the land in order to wipeout mankind, the following analysis deals with **just the water needed to cover the land** and not raise the ocean levels, i.e. the amount of water required by an **asteroid hitting our oceans to cover earth's landmass**:

As to earth's **landmass**, the average elevation is 2,600 feet, so we would only need an **average of 3,600 feet** of water to cover all of the landmass at an **average depth** of 1,000 feet. Since mountainous areas would displace water volume, the amount of water on the land to reach a level of 29,000 feet would still only require an **average elevation increase** of **3,600 feet** of water. Keep in mind that the mountains would displace water volume. In other words, the water would race up the mountainsides and "not fill up" the mountain's volume. An analogous situation is the lesser amount of water required to completely fill up your bathtub when you are sitting in it, as opposed to when you are not. (Yes, in this analogy you are the mountain and the bigger you are the less water is needed.)

Given that the earth's landmass is only 28% of the earth, which is just **39%** of the ocean's surface, because the ocean is 72% of the earth (28%/72% = **39%**), it would only require an amount of water equal to just **10%** of the ocean's water (3,600/13,740 x 39% = **10%**) to be able to cover the entire landmass by an **average** height of 1,000 feet of water.

Asteroids hitting our oceans would only be required to **temporarily** displace 10% of the ocean's water in order to cover the landmass of earth to an **average elevation of 3,600 feet** and then the water would slowly drain back into the oceans. This temporary displacement of water would cause the ocean's average level to drop by only **10%** or **1,374** feet (13,740 x 10% = **1,374**).

Keep in mind that in my example the entire landmass would be covered by an **average** of 1,000 feet of water, but this is just an **average depth**, so the lowlands may be covered by 3,000 feet of water while the summit of Mount Everest may only have just 50 feet of water washing over it.

Relative to the actual level of the rising water on land, please keep in mind that the water would not necessarily have to top the tallest mountains, as virtually all of the people (99.9%) would have lived well below 6,000 feet, primarily for the cultivation, irrigation and harvesting of their crops. And I believe it safe to say that 100% of the people lived well below 13,000 feet due to the oxygen being so extremely thin above that elevation that it causes altitude sickness, not to mention the likelihood of freezing conditions. Please note that temperatures drop by 3 degrees for every 1,000 feet of elevation, so there would be a 39-degree drop in temperature going from sea level to an elevation of 13,000 feet (13 x 3 = 39).

Lastly, I doubt that anyone could have safely reached Mount Everest's summit of 29,000 feet in those primitive days, especially with a tsunami chasing him or her at 500 to 600 miles per hour, unless however it was some of the evil Nephilim (giants) who survived the flood.

Can you imagine the shear power of 10% of the ocean's waters rushing over the lands with multiple waves of over 1,000 feet high racing up the mountainsides at speeds upwards of 500 to 600 miles per hour (the estimated speed of known tsunamis)?

Consequently, this is a very credible scenario in comparison to earth's sea level increasing to 29,000 feet around the entire globe, which would be **absolutely impossible**. Regardless of whether it was caused by God, the gods or Mother Nature, I am convinced that this is the only way it could have logically happened. And based on the analysis above it may not have even required 10% of the ocean's waters because of the demographics of the population, i.e. living well below 13,000 feet, which would give more credibility to how some of the Nephilim were able to survive, i.e. by only needing to go above 13,000 feet and not 29,000 feet.

As to the Bible's version, where would all of the water come from to cause a rise in sea level to 29,000 feet? The volume of water required from any amount of rain would not be possible (remember that rain is a recycled event of all waters on earth as a result of evaporation and condensation). Also, keep in mind that at the end of the last ice age the ocean level only increased by 400 feet and scientists are in agreement that if all of earth's ice melted today it would only cause a 216 foot rise in sea level. But who is to say, as anything would be possible with God, but if it really was God that destroyed mankind, then He certainly could have simply commanded it with the blink of an eye, right? Obviously, God would not be constrained by either logic, the laws of physics, or of any other laws of nature for that matter. And of course God could have also caused the Great Flood by having asteroids hit our oceans as well.

If this was a local flood, then a single asteroid hitting the Indian Ocean might very well have caused the flood; but if it was just local, then was the rest of the world's population being ignored for their sinful ways?

Are we really so self-absorbed to believe that we were God's first and only creation of an intelligent life form in the entire universe? As stated earlier, astrophysicists believe that there exists in excess of a hundred billion galaxies, so not only is it very likely but almost a certainty that other intelligent life forms exist in the universe.

It is said in the Bible that God created earth in 6 days and that He rested on the seventh day, but it didn't say what He did for the next 4.5 billion years until the stories were recorded in the Bible. In any event, if we are that self-absorbed then we should be really upset that God actually created dinosaurs millions of years before He decided to create us. Why the dinosaurs first and why were they subsequently destroyed by an **asteroid**? Was their creation and subsequent destruction evidence of yet another "mistake" or "experiment" of fallible gods, or just part of God's master plan? If it was the latter, then what purpose did it serve in His master plan?

It has been a widely accepted theory since 1980 that a huge 6-mile wide **asteroid** hit Mexico's Yucatan Peninsula about 65 million years ago as evidenced by a gigantic crater 110 miles wide. **Doesn't it appear that "God's" MO (Method of Operation) or choice of a weapon of mass destruction may, in fact, have been an asteroid?** Interestingly the biggest threat to earth in the future other than a nuclear war is thought to be a wide range of asteroids that are coming our way. Fortunately, most of the large ones are not being drawn into earth's gravitational pull, but many pose a great risk nonetheless.

I find it interesting that the dinosaurs lived for about 185 million years from about 250 million years ago until they became extinct about 65 million years ago. In contrast humans have only been around for about 200 thousand years, so based on longevity the dinosaurs were by far the dominant species on earth without question.

Is it possible that God destroyed the dinosaurs to make way for intelligent beings, which He knew could not coexist with dinosaurs, as they would eat our lunch, or more correctly, we would be their lunch? If so, then why did He then wait millions of years before creating us? Of course one could always say that millions of years is just a blink of the eye for God, right?

In any case, after the dinosaurs were destroyed 65 million years ago by an asteroid, scientists have estimated that it would have required up to 20 million years for earth to recover its ecosystem by a natural process to allow for humans to exist. **This time frame would still have allowed God to create our "ancestors"**

up to as much as 45 million years ago on earth or possibly millions of more years ago on another planet.

Therefore, God could have created these "ancestors" millions of years ago, and since they would have been an intelligent life form, they would have developed very quickly just like we have. Just imagine how far advanced we could be in the next thousand or even in the next million years or more from now. Is it possible that it was these "ancestors", which could have developed far beyond where we are today, that became our gods? Is it possible that after millions of years living on earth that the earth became uninhabitable, which required them to find refuge on another planet? Might there have been a nuclear war on earth between the gods possibly millions of years ago that resulted in their demise or exodus to another planet with the total destruction of any proof whatsoever of their existence here on earth? They certainly would have had the developmental intellectual time to exploit interplanetary travel.

Alternatively, with earth having undergone a number of life-extinguishing climate changes over the millennium, could this be yet another reason for their refuge to another planet just like some are predicting for our future based on our over-population, pollution and global warming? If life on earth as we know it were ended today, would there be any proof of our having lived on earth a thousand or thousands of years from now? Absolutely everything that we have built would have decayed to dust over many millennia and all that would be left for future explorers of earth to discover would be the pyramids and stone structures that were built by our "ancestors". **There would be absolutely no proof of our existence whatsoever.** Is it possible that history may be repeating itself?

Relative to time since the creation of the universe, humans, as we know them, have only existed for a microsecond, or just 0.00005% of the total time. As an example, in a 24-hour day our existence would only represent just 2 seconds of time, so within the vastness of the other 23 hours, 59 minutes and 58 seconds of time I believe that our history, as we have been taught, will some day be totally rewritten...so stay tuned.

If our "ancestors" were God's first or earlier intelligent creations on another planet and if these "ancestors" visited earth as "astronauts", which were viewed by "earthlings" as gods, then **could it possibly be that they were an instrument of God in our creation?** If so, then possibly we were created in "their image" by the sharing of their DNA with the evolving earthlings (apes or other primitive life forms), which was the missing link. **If and only if** this is what happened, did **we essentially become them**? In other words, are we a hybrid of these ancient astronauts and subsequently we are destine to achieve the same level of technology advancement that they attained? Our technology has actually been occurring at an astounding and undeniable rate.

If the forgoing assumption is true, then what would our relationship be with God? It would obviously be a "second hand" relationship at best. Would this mean that we are too far removed from God that He obviously knows of our existence but it may be a hands-off relationship? Those of faith have a belief in prayer as a way to communicate with God, but is it possible that the good feeling that we derive from our faith and prayer is simply a form of meditation, which has a very calming affect on our state of mind? Would this also explain why not all prayers are answered and why bad things happen to good people? Nonetheless, I believe that the power of prayer is the power of positive thinking, which gives one a sense of comfort by placing difficult matters in God's hands, so there is absolutely no downside; and who knows, maybe God really is listening, right? **{"It is the mark of an educated mind to be able to entertain a thought without accepting it." Aristotle}**

As previously stated, if we take this hypothetical thinking full circle we must ask ourselves the question; namely, **if our ancient ancestors or extraterrestrial astronauts via their DNA created us, then do we have a soul?** In other words, do subsequent "secondhand" creations of intelligent beings with the DNA of God's first creation have the "soul gene" in it? **I believe that anyone with a Conscience and Free Will with the inherit ability to distinguish between right and wrong would have a God given soul.**

The following is a consolidated summary of unanswered questions regarding God:

Would the **real God** require or even want a means of transportation to transport anyone that He wished, i.e. Enoch?

Also, would the **real God** have allowed Enoch's people to be killed because they were too close to His "fiery chariot" upon taking off?

Would the **real God** have needed or even wanted help from anyone, i.e. the 200 "angels" or the "sons of God" that were with Him for some reason and subsequently came to earth?

Would the **real God** have known and then been able to stop the "bad angels" from descending to earth?

Would the **real God** have designed the Ark of the Covenant that could accidently kill anyone, i.e. Uzzah?

Would the **real God** have created a flood that would kill millions of humans and animals, and yet somehow allow some of the evil Nephilim to survive, since He could have simply destroyed whomever or whatever He wanted with the blink of an eye?

Who Is the Real God?

Would the **real God** be concerned about humans building anything, i.e. the Tower of Babel? Additionally, would the **real God** have known that confusing our language would only last a relatively short period of time before we would once again be united and accomplish technological feats that would make the tower look like a step stool?

Would the **real God** have allowed the "righteous" wife of Lot to be killed during the destruction of Sodom and Gomorrah?

Would the **real God** require a means of transportation to travel to and from earth, i.e. Ezekiel's vision?

Would the **real God** have allowed humans to see His face without killing them if He wanted? And would the **real God** even have offered a reason or an excuse of why we couldn't?

Would the **real God** have made any mistakes whatsoever as stated in the Bible, i.e. admitting that He had made a mistake in creating humans and not being able to successfully kill all of the Nephilim in the Great Flood?

The ultimate and exciting conclusion of <u>Who Is The Real God?</u> is squarely in your hands, which is where it rightfully belongs, so it is up to you and you alone to make your own informed conclusion.

To see my personal conclusion please read the Epilogue, but first the next two chapters explore "The Meaning of Life" and "Heaven".

CHAPTER 21

THE MEANING OF LIFE

As to **the meaning of life, which was my original quest for knowledge and enlightenment,** I offer the following:

I believe that the eyewitness Bible stories of Jesus Christ (Son of God) are very unique in that not only did He prophesize His own death and resurrection like no other, but He fulfilled the prophesy and also performed a number of miracles, not the least of which was raising Lazarus from the dead as chronicled in the Bible. As to His own resurrection, His body didn't just disappear from the tomb as some could say (grave robbers), but His reappearance was the proof as evidenced by witnesses, including Thomas (doubting Thomas). **Hence, His reappearance is the de-facto proof of His resurrection.**

Even though the chronicles of the life of Jesus in the New Testament were 2,000 years ago, it wasn't like most of the stories in the Old

Testament, which were many thousands of years earlier dating back to the Creation of the Universe and Adam and Eve. The Old Testament was written between 1,600 and 400 BC and chronicled events based on **oral history.** Conversely, with compelling eyewitnesses and the existence of the written word, the life of Jesus is **relatively speaking** a current event. In fact, the New Testament was written between 50 and 90 AD and Jesus died about 33AD, therefore it was written between 17 to 57 years after His death, so **relative** to all of the stories in the Bible, the stories of the life of Jesus are **relatively speaking** almost contemporaneous.

Also, Jesus practiced **love and compassion** unlike the war mongering gods and most of the so-called prophets of God. He said that **He has a plan for our lives**, which centers on a relationship with Him and for that relationship to be possible He had to die on the cross for our sins. He and He alone epitomize a **loving God**, and as our Savior we need to follow His example. **Isn't this the type of God that everyone would want?**

Every day it is becoming more and more clear that we are losing our way, as it seems that more and more of our religious beliefs, or God's rules are being replaced by man's human rights. This is the beginning of the end because in order to perpetuate this heresy (Godlessness), **we must first reject God**, and unfortunately, we are headed in that direction at an alarming speed with the removal of both prayer in our schools and God's Ten Commandments from the public squares for example. I believe that the cause or reason behind this is the embracing of a new and ever growing creed to be **tolerant**, which not only sounds good but actually sounds great and clearly fits in with loving your neighbor as yourself; **however**, if being "tolerant" means **the acceptance of and the embracing of absolutely everything including evil (which I believe it clearly does)**, then we are becoming Godless people, just like the lawless people who were wiped out by the Great Flood.

Unfortunately, it only takes a small minority to control and suppress a belief in God due to our rules of democracy based on the principle of **the separation of church and state**.

Therefore, the best that any of us can do is to use our God given intellect plus faith, and hopefully with the grace of God we will find guidance in how to properly live our lives. It defies reason that God would create us without a purpose or a meaning of life.

In my **personal quest for the meaning of life**, I have concluded that it is to **live in peace and happiness**, which is only possible **by living in the here and now (present)** and **by loving one another by showing compassion for each other** as taught by Jesus. Living in the present is the only place to find happiness and by helping others we receive a tremendous amount pleasure, which I explain in my book **<u>Taming Your Inner Monkey</u>**. How great would our society (world) be if we all, or at least most of us, practiced **love and compassion for each other**? As I said in my book regarding practicing compassion, **"try it you will like it, guaranteed. No I don't guarantee it but your brain does as that is how our brains are hard wired"**. This is exactly what Jesus taught us, so yet another reason to embrace Him and follow His example. In the Sermon on the Mount, Jesus gave us assurance that, "Blessed are the merciful, for they shall obtain mercy." This can be restated as, **"Blessed are the compassionate, for they shall obtain compassion."**

Living in peace and happiness and showing compassion for each other will give us pleasure and make us feel better about ourselves for doing good work, but **it will not gain us Heaven**. The next chapter will explain what is required, which may surprise you but in a very positive way.

CHAPTER 22

HEAVEN

This book would not be complete without talking about Heaven, so not being shy about avoiding potentially controversial topics I will give it my best shot.

Ancient scripture speaks extensively about those who came from Heaven to earth or ascended to Heaven from earth (a lot of coming and going). However, I believe that "Heaven" was only a reference to the **infinite skies**, which because it was **physically inaccessible to man** was simply referred to as Heaven in possibly a mystical or spiritual way because the "gods" came from the skies. I do not believe that it was necessarily a reference to a final destination after death for those who were "good people", i.e. **less sinful** than others (yes, God grades on a curve).

So where do we go when we die? Well, many Christians who believe in Jesus Christ also believe that only those who accept Jesus as being their Savior will be saved and consequently go to Heaven. Even though I believe in Jesus Christ as our Savior, I must confess that it seems more than a little unfair for those "good people", who have lived and died--without an opportunity to experience the teachings of Jesus--to not be allowed to go to Heaven. As an example, where did the "good people" go that died prior to the coming of Jesus Christ? Also, there was at least a 1500-year delay in getting the Word out after the death of Jesus due to both the lack of the printing press and the logistics in distributing it around the world, not to mention the time to translate it into many languages. In fact, the earliest that Columbus could have brought the Bible to the "new world" would have been in 1492 and Cortez to South America in 1519, so it begs the question: **Where did hundreds of millions if not billions of "good people" go after they died?**

Are all non-Christians specifically excluded from Heaven? I believe that most people are good people regardless of their religious belief, or no belief at all, so if they happen to be our friends then not being able to see them in Heaven would make **Heaven not as perfect** as one would wish it to be, which I find impossible to accept.

Okay, now for the good news, the Catholic Church actually talks about this and essentially says that **Jesus wants everyone to be saved, even non-Catholics, non- Christians, etc., and everyone that has ever existed. Basically, it is enough that we follow our conscience.** And as I had stated earlier, **it is our God given conscience with free will that allows us to decide between good and evil, so it will actually be "our actions" that will ultimately be judged by God.**

Being a member of any religious organization will obviously give us **guidance** as to how best to live our lives, but in lieu of any religious guidance, **"let your conscience be your guide"**. Having said that, everyone owes it to himself or herself to exercise their intellectual curiosity by **sincerely seeking to learn about God and the teachings of Jesus** and hopefully follow His example. **"Seeking" is the path to faith regardless of one's conscious acceptance of God; however, one must actually seek information or enlightenment.**

In support of what I have said in the preceding paragraphs, I offer the following:

In **The Light of Faith**, which was started by **Pope Benedict** and completed by **Pope Francis**, it says: "Because faith is a way, it also has to do with the lives of those men and women who, **though not believers**, nonetheless **desire to believe and continue to seek**. To the extent that they are sincerely open to love and **set out with whatever light they can find**, they are already, even without knowing it, on the path to faith. They strive to act as if God exists..."

When asked about **"Obeying One's Conscience"**, **Pope Francis** responded by saying, "You ask me if the God of Christians forgives one who doesn't believe and doesn't seek the faith. Premise that--and it's the fundamental thing--the mercy of God has no limits if one turns to him with a sincere and contrite heart; **the question for one who doesn't believe in God lies in obeying one's conscience. To listen to and obey it means, in fact, to decide in face of what is perceived as good or evil**".

Additionally, Pope Francis said, "I have a dogmatic certainty: **God is in every person's life**. God is in everyone's life. Even if the life of a person has been a disaster, even if vices, drugs or anything else destroys it—God is in this person's life. You can, you must try to seek God in every human life. Although the life of a person is a land full of thorns and weeds, there is always a space in which the good seed can grow".

Basically, it is my understanding that **obeying one's conscience is what God will take account of in granting forgiveness, so Pope Francis is saying that the conscience is the final judge to whom God will submit to himself for final judgment. Basically, the human conscience is the determinative factor for God's forgiveness.**

We are all children of God and if by God's limitless grace even atheists are redeemed by Christ, then why go to Mass? Cardinal Dolan of New York answered that question by saying, "Look, you don't go to Mass to win heaven. **You go to ask God for help to get you there**. **You go to Mass to thank him for being such a great God** that he wants you to spend eternity with him. That's why you go to Mass. You don't go to win heaven, because you can't earn it—it's a gift. He wants to give it to all of us." **Essentially, you go to Mass or church etc. to seek guidance in how to live your life and to give thanks to God.**

I would like to believe the stories of people who had "flat lined" and then were revived to tell their story of being in Heaven and saw their friends and relatives that had previously died. **These stories are very heartwarming and include feelings of serenity, peace and love**; however, most if not all accounts describe people they see in their "recognizable human form".

If Heaven was that great wouldn't we all have young vibrant bodies and not the ones that were last "recognizable" as an old grandfather or grandmother? If I were to be so lucky to go to Heaven, then when my youngest grandson joins me he would not be able to recognize me as a young man because he only knew what I looked like when I was in my 70's and older. Oops, I forgot about nametags, problem solved! No, seriously an all-powerful God would obviously allow us to **see and recognize a loved one as we remembered them** despite their actual form in Heaven, should it be spiritual or otherwise.

EPILOGUE

In thinking about publishing this book, which I had researched for eight years and completed writing a year ago, I had second and third thoughts, so **I sat on it for an entire year while weighing whether it would do more harm than good**. I had gradually and leisurely conducted my "research" **solely for my own edification or enlightenment** and never even thought of writing this book until I became convinced that others, especially agnostics and atheists with an open mind, might find this information to be not only thought provoking but also compelling.

The ultimate Creator of both the universe and the gods must have been the one and only God. In connecting the dots one must qualify the ancient recorded accounts of "God" as not being the actions of an infallible God, but rather the actions of the fallible gods. These gods may or may not have had a hand in our creation; but they certainly had a hand in giving us knowledge. If and

only if we are a product of their creation, then the only answer to why God would **"allow this to happen"** is that as an intelligent life form they would have had a God given **soul and a conscience with the free will to decide between right and wrong**, which by God's own design would **preclude His involvement in their free will**. God's prior creation(s), i.e. "the gods", were far superior to us in their knowledge and technological abilities, so was it actually these gods who were essentially "playing God" relative to our subsequent creation? As stated earlier, we actually have the ability to do that right now; however, moral and governmental laws preclude us from cloning or creating test tube babies at least for now on our planet.

It will be our **conscience and free will** that will ultimately dictate what we end up doing and I doubt that God will step in and prevent our actions any more than He would have with the actions of His prior creation(s) of intelligent life forms. **Did God prevent Cain from murdering Abel?** This also aids us with an understanding of **why God "allows bad things to happen"**, like murders, abortions and rape for example. In other words, **God will not stop us from exercising our free will** even if it is something that is wrong. This begs an extremely provocative question; **if and only if the gods with their free will** had a hand in our creation, **then were they wrong for having created us?**

I started this book by saying that **"I believe that it takes an infinite amount of faith to believe that there is no God than to believe that there is a God"**, so now that we are at the end of the book I must also say that **I believe that it takes an infinite amount of faith to believe that the actions of "God" as described in the Bible were about God's actions than to believe that those actions were of imposter gods, i.e. extraterrestrial astronauts (aka angels, fallen angels, sons of God or ancient ancestors), which I believe were God's first or earlier intelligent creation(s) prior to the creation of humans on earth.** The Bible speaks of them as if they were Godlike, but as the Biblical stories go, they were far from it and, in fact, were more like fallible humans.

As stated several times previously, are we really so self-absorbed as not to keep open the possibility that we may not have been God's first and only choice for an intelligent life form?

The only remaining question that I had was whether the god's actions were **directed or approved by God**? I believe the answer to that question is an **emphatic no**, as a loving and all-powerful God would never have been complicit in many of their actions with perhaps the **possible exception of their having a hand in our creation, if and only if that is what happened**. As one of God's prior creations these beings would have had a **soul and a conscience with the free will to decide between right and wrong** and their actions or choices will ultimately be judged by God just like ours will.

Information about the author can be seen online by going to Amazon.com and entering his first book's title: How To Succeed In Business By Really Trying / Michael Hill
His other book, Taming Your Inner Monkey is available both in paperback or Kindle by going online to Amazon or Barnes and Noble.

www.ingramcontent.com/pod-product-compliance
Lightning Source LLC
Chambersburg PA
CBHW040311050426
42450CB00019B/3457